Confronting Prejudice

Lesbian and gay issues in social work education

Janette Logan
Sheila Kershaw
Kate Karban
Sue Mills
Joy Trotter
Margo Sinclair

Published by
Arena
Ashgate Publishing Limited
Gower House
Croft Road
Aldershot
Hants GU11 3HR
England

Ashgate Publishing Company
Old Post Road
Brookfield
Vermont 05036
USA

British Library Cataloguing in Publication Data

Confronting prejudice: lesbian and gay issues
  in social work education
  1. Social service and sex   2. Discrimination
  in employment   3. Gays – Employment
  I. Logan, Janette
  361.3'0866

Library of Congress Catalog Card Number: 96-85237

ISBN 1 85742 360 7 (paperback)
ISBN 1 85742 359 3 (hardback)

Typeset in Palatino by Raven Typesetters Ltd, Chester.
Printed and bound in Great Britain by Hartnolls Ltd, Bodmin.

Contents

Foreword

I have pleasure in providing the foreword to this publication, high-lighting as it does an important and often neglected area within social work education and practice.

CCETSW's equal opportunities policy (adopted in 1989) stated that the 'Central Council for Education and Training in Social Work will seek to ensure that in all dimensions of its activity – as an employer, validating body, and in its development work – individuals are not unfairly disadvantaged on the grounds of age, gender, disability, language (including sign language), race, ethnic origin, nationality, sexual orientation, social class or religion.' A revised equal opportunities policy statement was approved in May 1995.

Early in 1993 a piece of work was commissioned to make a reality of this commitment in respect to sexual orientation. This led to a report to CCETSW's education and training group, which made a number of recommendations.

One of these was that regional offices should be encouraged, through their equal opportunities action plans, to develop the sharing of good practice, and support the development of practical resources with others in their region.

Simultaneously, a programme to promote good practice in the teaching of child care in the Diploma in Social Work was being undertaken in CCETSW's Northern England office. An opportunity arose to link the two activities.

Following a series of workshops which took place between 1993 and 1994, a group of social work teachers and practitioners emerged, committed to raising the profile of lesbian and gay sexuality within social work education. The group developed proposals for this publication, with advisory help from this regional office, and applied to us for funding. I am happy that we were able to support them.

I commend this publication to you. It is intended to be a practical resource for all those involved in working with social work students. At the same time it will, I hope, stimulate debate and encourage a real acknowledgement of the needs of lesbian and gay students, educators and service users.

Brenda Toward, Head
Northern England CCETSW
January 1996

Acknowledgements

We are indebted to many colleagues, students and service users who have contributed both directly and indirectly to the material included in this publication.

We are particularly aware that we have not been able to find sources for all of the training material used. The spirit in which we have approached this book is one based on the view that materials need to be shared in order to develop sound anti-oppressive strategies which are owned by everyone.

We would like to thank Ruth Hall from CCETSW Northern England for her support and encouragement and tireless scrutiny to detail throughout the whole process.

Thank-you to Jackie Gilchrist, Wendy Marshall, John Hancox, Steve Myers and Sue Payne for their particular contributions.

Thank-you to Elaine Sammon for her endless patience in typing and re-typing this publication.

Thank-you to CCETSW for commissioning the publication and particularly to Brenda Toward (Head of CCETSW Northern England), for her continued support.

Thank-you to readers.

Value statement

In writing this book, we acknowledge that as a group of white non-disabled women – some lesbian, some heterosexual – we are a narrowly representative group and therefore do not reflect the diversities within contemporary society.

We do, however, acknowledge the need to recognise the complexities, connections and tensions of oppression and believe that no one area of oppression can be understood in isolation from all others, as Audre Lorde has said:

> To deal with one without even alluding to the other is to distort our commonality as well as our difference. (Lorde, 1984, p. 70)

Lesbian and gay issues cannot, therefore, be explored and understood in isolation from gender, religion, disability, class, race, and age. Our approach in addressing the issues is thus set within this wider context which recognises the inter-connectedness and non-hierarchical nature of the various forms of oppression.

Essentially our approach seeks to celebrate and value difference and the rich contribution it makes to our lives.

Glossary

Anti-oppressive practice   Seeking to empower service users and colleagues by recognising and challenging inequalities and oppression in all aspects of social work.

Bisexual   A man or woman who may have primary sexual and emotional relationships with either men or women. The term describes the individual, and not the relationship.

Closet   A term used by lesbians and gay men to denote that they are not able to be open about their identity in some or all aspects of their lives.

Come out   A term used by lesbians and gay men to mean being open about their identity in a particular situation, or more generally in their lives.

Discrimination   A word which has been used to denote any kind of choice or selection. It has more recently become a term to denote policy, practice or behaviour which is based on unfair treatment or prejudice shown to individuals or groups.

Gay   Derives from the twelfth century French Provençal word *Gai* – meaning courtly love between two men. The word is gender specific; however, it is sometimes used to describe *both* men and women who relate to people of the same sex. Lesbians often prefer to describe themselves separately. The term describes the person's identity, not the relationship.

Gender   Socially ascribed definition placed on male and female to create 'masculine' and 'feminine'.

Heterosexism   The set of assumptions and practices which serve to promote heterosexuality (relationships between women and men). Heterosexism as a system states that the only valid 'normal' and 'natural' relationships are heterosexual ones. Heterosexism penalises those who do not conform to heterosexuality and rewards those who do. Thus it is also an institutionalised form of discrimination, since all the institutions in society discriminate against those who are not heterosexual or who are in homosexual relationships.

Heterosexual   Women or men whose primary emotional and sexual relationships are with people of the opposite sex.

Homophobia   Irrational fear or hatred of lesbians or gay men which causes discrimination.

Homosexual   A more clinical term for describing either lesbians or gay men. Rarely used by lesbians or gay men themselves.

Ideology   A system of ideas or ways of thinking characteristic of a social group or an individual – usually based on particular values.

Internalised oppression   If individuals come to believe that the systematic mistreatment or misinformation about them is justified or true, they can be said to have internalised oppression. The term refers to any resulting beliefs or behaviour.

Lesbian   Derives from the Greek island of Lesbos where Sappho, a lesbian poet, lived in 600 BC. The word is gender specific. It refers to a woman who relates emotionally and sexually to other women. The definition refers to the woman herself, not to the relationship – so, for instance, a lesbian who is not currently in a relationship will still be a lesbian, while a bisexual woman in a relationship with a woman would not be regarded as a lesbian. Some lesbians also see the term as a political definition. Not all women who have sex with other women identify as lesbians, and not all lesbians are exclusively attracted to other women.

Oppression   'A complex term which relates to structural differences in power as well as to the personal experience of oppressing or being oppressed. It relates to race, gender, sexual orientation, age, disability, [class] as separate domains and as overlapping experiences' (Phillipson, 1992, p. 13). Oppression is supported and perpetuated by society's institutions.

Prejudice An attitude which is derived not from direct knowledge of the group or individuals concerned, but from some preconceived opinion or stereotype.

Queer As a noun, this usually refers to a man. As an adjective, it is characteristic of either men or women. The term is used negatively by those outside the gay community. Recently the word has been reclaimed by some gay men and lesbians as a term denoting distinction between heterosexual and gay lifestyles.

Sex Chromosomally imposed difference between being male and female.

Sexuality A complex term which includes sexual feelings, thoughts and behaviour relating to individuals, groups and organisations and is affected by social conditioning and the prevailing socio-political context.

Social construction A network of related ideas, images and values which build-up a *socially* derived picture of a human condition or characteristic, e.g. old age or disability.

Stereotype An allegedly agreed upon 'type' or caricature that attributes certain characteristics to individuals on the basis of the group to which they belong, or because of some genetic factor.

Purpose of the book

The purpose of this book is to bring lesbian and gay issues to the centre of the debate on anti-oppressive practice. It is intended to be an accessible and practical guide to the subject for all those involved in student learning and aims to provide practice teachers and educators with tools for helping students develop their understanding of the effects of heterosexism as well as strategies for positive practice. In order to attain the latter goal, we believe it is necessary to raise each individual's awareness and, where necessary, challenge assumptions. It is essential, therefore, that any teaching strategy incorporates a theoretical understanding of the subject with an examination of personal values, attitudes and experiences.

Our approach is encompassed in the words of Cherrie Moraga (1981):

> Failing to acknowledge the specificity of oppression, ranking them so that some are more important than others, attempting to deal with oppression from a purely theoretical base without an emotional, heartfelt grappling with some of the source of our own oppression, without naming the enemy within ourselves and outside of us, no authentic, non-hierarchical connection among oppressed groups can take place. (Cited in Phillipson, 1992, pp. 13–14)

As a group of educators and practice teachers committed to putting lesbian and gay issues on the agenda, we have had the opportunity in writing this book to share experiences and ideas and to discuss and debate questions among ourselves. Furthermore, for some of us, these issues are real life challenges which we have to deal with in our personal and professional lives. We do not have all the answers, nor can we, in a text of this nature, examine the issues raised in sufficient

xvii

depth. The complexities surrounding 'coming out', for example, are so profoundly individual that we must not attempt to provide the answers. It is important to recognise that every individual's experience is unique. As a group of white women, we cannot reflect the experiences of black lesbians or gay men, for whom racism, religion and culture will make their experience markedly different from our own.

Our intention in writing this book is therefore to make the subject matter visible in the broadest sense, and in so doing, to contribute to the development of good policy and practice with lesbian and gay service users and colleagues.

Whilst the book is focused primarily at the education and training of social work students, we hope it will also be useful for practitioners who are developing good policy and practice both in relation to service users and agency employees.

The structure of the books is as follows.

Chapter 1 presents the contextual framework, raising important issues about the ways in which lesbians and gay men are marginalised in society and the subsequent reflection in social work education and practice.

Chapter 2 details the legal framework within which social workers and probation officers operate. The chapter draws attention to some of the tensions and dilemmas facing practitioners attempting to develop anti-discriminatory and anti-oppressive practice with lesbian and gay service users.

Chapter 3 presents a foundation for developing non-homophobic and anti-heterosexist practice within the Diploma in Social Work. The chapter also raises important issues which need to be addressed both within academic institutions and the practice learning environment.

Chapter 4 focuses on teaching and learning strategies to facilitate students' learning in relation to anti-discriminatory, anti-oppressive practice with lesbians and gay service users. Developing competence within an approach which integrates knowledge, skills and values is emphasised.

Chapter 5 concerns the assessment of competence in both academic and practice settings and argues that explicit requirements are necessary to draw attention to lesbian and gay issues.

A model of good practice in working with lesbians and gay men is proposed in Chapter 6. This offers a range of strategies and suggestions which can be incorporated into existing policies and procedures.

Part 2 of the book presents a range of teaching and training materials which can be used flexibly and adapted to reflect a range of individual or group needs:

- Individual practice teaching sessions, case study material and exercises can be introduced into the supervision sessions to provide practice learning opportunities for students.
- The material can be developed to offer half- or one-day workshops either within the practice learning or academic environment.
- The material can be used within the academic curriculum either in discrete modules and/or to permeate teaching which addresses anti-discriminatory/anti-oppressive practice in the broadest sense.
- The material can also be utilised for practice teacher training.

Part 1

Background

1 Setting the context

Introduction

There has been, over the last twenty years, an increasing awareness of inequalities in society resulting in legislative reform, particularly in relation to race and gender, which has aimed to alleviate the discrimination experienced by people on an individual level. Equal opportunities policies, with their explicit commitment to develop anti-discriminatory policies and practices for employers and service users, are now common place in agencies, and the Race Relations Act (1976) and the Sex Discrimination Act (1975) have provided legal mandates against the discrimination of black people and women. This is not to deny that these groups continue to be oppressed on a societal level; however, the discrimination they experience on an individual level is at least being addressed. Similarly, the discrimination experienced by other groups – for example, by disabled and older people – is increasingly being recognised. The situation is very different, however, for lesbians and gay men, and the belief that it is right to discriminate on the grounds of sexual orientation is not only widespread but is also sanctioned by the law.

Discrimination against lesbians and gay men can take the form of homophobia or the more common, subtle indirect pervasiveness of heterosexism with its assumption that heterosexuality is the norm. Whilst this is often unintentional, it is however no less oppressive:

> Social workers and clients live in a world that hates, fears and is fascinated by homosexuality ... social work ... takes place in this context. (Cosis Brown, 1992, p. 216)

It cannot be assumed that social work and its institutions are immune

3

to this dominant ideology, for as the National Association of Local Government Officers pointed out:

> although social work is traditionally a caring profession this by no means guarantees that social service staff have sympathetic attitudes towards lesbians and gay men or that departments are prepared to develop positive policies. (NALGO, 1992, p. 18)

Research in the US has highlighted the incidence of homophobia among social workers (De Crescenzo and McGill, 1978; Wisniewski and Toomey, 1987); and closer to home, Trenchard and Warren (1984) reported the prevalence of anti-gay and lesbian attitudes in schools and colleges. There is no evidence to suggest that the situation is any different in universities and other higher education establishments where social workers are trained.

Social work courses are now directed to identify and challenge issues of inequality and structural oppression (CCETSW, Paper 30, 1995a); however, as Bremner and Hillin pointed out:

> lesbian and gay oppression is generally not addressed in social work training and is probably the one least understood by workers. (1993, p. 28)

As a result of this lack of understanding, the traditional pathologising of lesbians and gay men still acts as a powerful influence on social work courses; and much social work training is directly homophobic (Cosis Brown, 1992). The consequences of this are far reaching, affecting both students and tutors on social work courses who may be gay or lesbian, as well as having profound implications for service users and service delivery.

In relation to service users, McMillan has highlighted the heterosexism of much of social work practice:

> Sexuality at the point of assessment is rarely if ever addressed in this sense ... but generally with a strong heterosexual bias. Questions concerning marriage, numbers of children and more poignantly whether the client is a bachelor or spinster still rear their ugly heads on certain forms within social service departments to this day. (McMillan, 1989, p. 31)

It is now acknowledged that at least 10 per cent of the population are lesbian or gay; yet this is ignored by social work professionals (Dulaney and Kelly, 1982). The result is that many lesbian or gay service users are discriminated against either indirectly by remaining invisible (Hillin, 1985) or directly by being denied services that are appropriate to their needs.

A recent survey carried out by the National Institute for Social Workers was concerned with identifying the causes of stress suffered by social workers; and it is perhaps not surprising that sexual orientation featured in their findings:

> It is regrettable that such a high proportion of staff in a caring profession may be affected by what must be a climate of fear and prejudice in the work place, and it certainly does not bode well for the way lesbian and gay clients are received. (NISW, 1995)

The context of oppression

Social work draws upon the theoretical perspectives of the social sciences, with sociological and psychological theory providing students with explanations to deepen their understanding of human behaviour. Unfortunately, when considering lesbian and gay issues, such texts are steeped in the deviancy theory, with its emphasis on individual pathology.

Whilst the eurocentric and sexist assumptions implicit in much of traditional theory are increasingly being challenged (Dominelli and Mcleod, 1989; Hanmer and Statham, 1988; Ahmed, 1990; Ely and Denney, 1987), there remains, however, a relative silence about the pervasive heterosexism of these works.

There is clearly a need to review and reconstruct the traditional theories informing social work practice. However, whilst there may be an absence of positive perspectives on lesbian and gay issues in mainstream social work literature, there is an increasing body of knowledge and theory which challenges the deviancy perspective (Wilkinson and Kitzinger, 1993; Weeks, 1989, 1991; Kitzinger, 1987; Caplan, 1987). Whilst this work currently exists on the fringe of sociology and psychology, it is imperative that it is recognised and utilised alongside the more traditional texts. There is also much to learn from the rich vein of fiction devoted to lesbian and gay experiences, which at one time may not have been considered suitable for the purposes of academic study and professional training.

However, while there may be a paucity of literature which positively addresses lesbian and gay issues, there is now a well-developed body of knowledge and theory which recognises the nature and reproduction of oppression and discrimination (Thompson, 1993; Webb and Tossell, 1991); and an understanding of lesbian and gay issues should be located in this wider theoretical framework. Developed largely by black and feminist writers (Dominelli and McLeod, 1989;

Hanmer and Statham, 1988; Ely and Denney, 1987), the theory about oppression has to be understood in terms of the structural differences in power as well as the personal experiences of oppressing or being oppressed. Whilst it is important to recognise the universal features of oppression, it is also important to acknowledge its unique and specific characteristics, e.g. of gender, race, disability, sexual orientation and so on. Numerous definitions of oppression have been formulated; however, we consider the following definition particularly helpful:

> Oppression is the process by which groups or individuals with ascribed or achieved power (the oppressors) unjustly limit the lives, experiences and/or opportunities of groups or individuals with less power (the oppressed). Oppression is supported and perpetuated by society's institutions. (NCVS, 1989, cited in Ward and Mullender, 1991, p. 23)

The institutionalised nature of oppression does not have to be explicitly repressive, rather it is manifested in a variety of subtle forms, moderating and containing conflict and defining what is seen as 'normal' and 'acceptable' through, for example, the working of the law, the media and the educational system (Ward and Mullender, 1991).

An understanding of oppression therefore must incorporate a number of layers, as illustrated in Figure 1.1. Figure 1.2 shows diagrammatically how discrimination and inequality are maintained.

It is also important to understand the correlation between various forms of oppression and the impact of multiple oppression, as Dominelli has succinctly pointed out:

> Oppression can occur along any number of dimensions. Oppression on the basis of race, gender, disability, age and sexual orientation is central to our present society which is permeated by relations of domination and subordination. Individuals experiencing oppression through a number of these dimensions experience them simultaneously, not one by one. (1988, pp. 158–9)

It is essential, therefore, when considering different forms of oppression, to understand and confront them together, for to do otherwise would result in the creation of an unhelpful and misleading hierarchy.

Developments in social work education

There have been significant developments in both social work education and practice during the 1990s. Social workers are now directed to

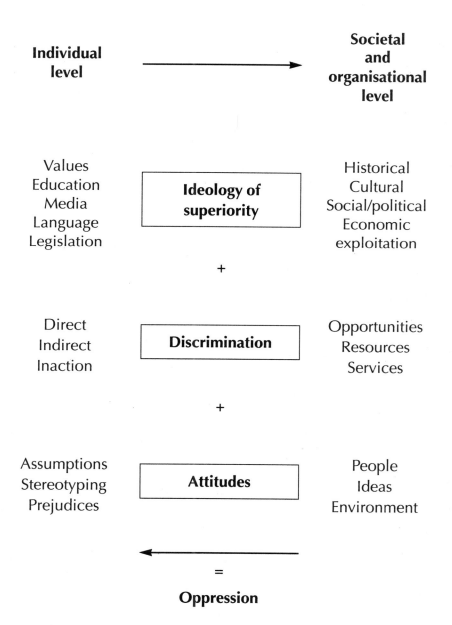

Figure 1.1   A model of oppression
Source: Derived from A.K. Ohri & Associates, 1989 (unpublished)

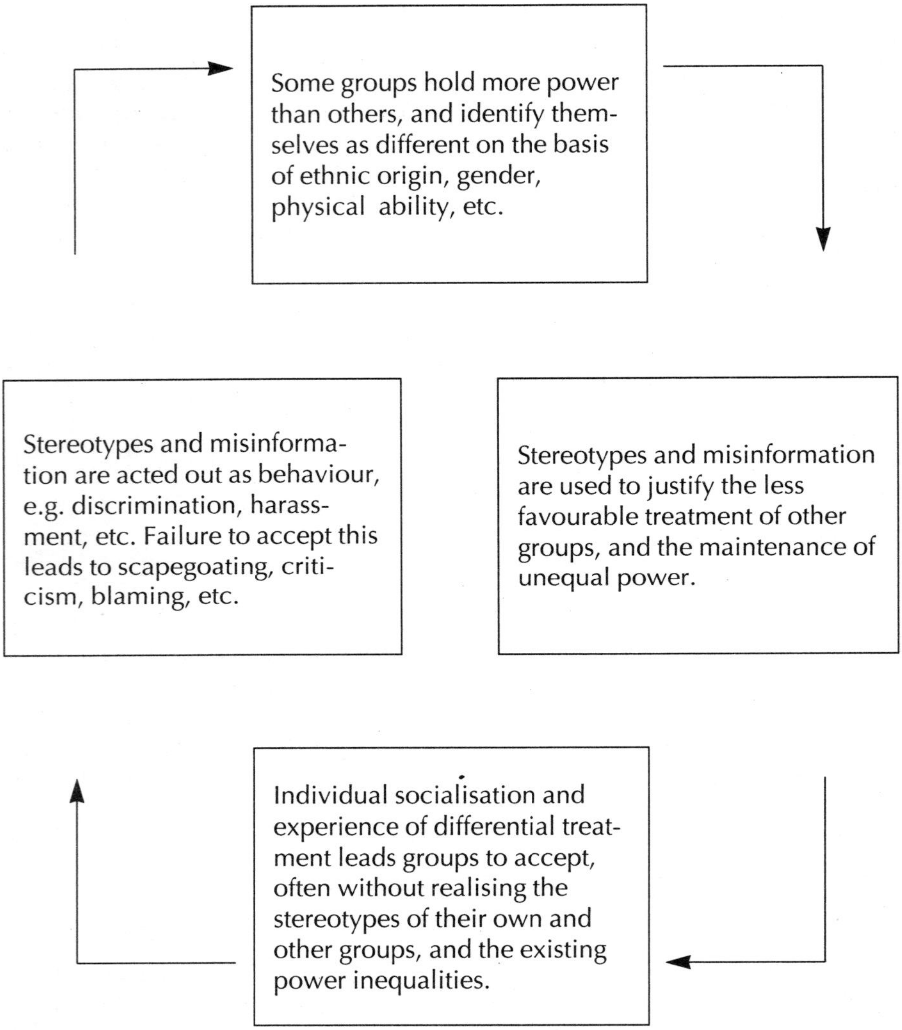

Some groups hold more power than others, and identify themselves as different on the basis of ethnic origin, gender, physical ability, etc.

Stereotypes and misinformation are acted out as behaviour, e.g. discrimination, harassment, etc. Failure to accept this leads to scapegoating, criticism, blaming, etc.

Stereotypes and misinformation are used to justify the less favourable treatment of other groups, and the maintenance of unequal power.

Individual socialisation and experience of differential treatment leads groups to accept, often without realising the stereotypes of their own and other groups, and the existing power inequalities.

Figure 1.2   How discrimination and inequality are maintained
Source: Derived from A.K. Ohri & Associates, 1989 (unpublished)

work in an anti-discriminatory and anti-oppressive way, with the concepts of empowerment and partnership being central to good practice (CCETSW, 1995a). The emphasis on competencies also marked a new departure, aimed at setting a minimum standard of 'good enough practice'. A major review of CCETSW Paper 30 has raised professional concerns about the strength of its value base; however, the notion of the integration of anti-discriminatory values into practice remains. The revised edition of Paper 30 states that the competent social worker must:

> Identify, analyse and take action to counter discrimination, racism, disadvantage, inequality and injustice, using strategies appropriate to role and context; and, practise in a manner that does not stigmatise or disadvantage . . . . (CCETSW, 1995a, p. 4)

The paper also emphasises the need for students to identify and question their own values and prejudices, stressing the importance of respecting and valuing uniqueness and diversity.

Within professional discourse, anti-discriminatory and anti-oppressive practice are used interchangeably; however, it is important to be clear about terminology, for there is a fundamental difference between the two. The definitions offered by Julia Phillipson are particularly useful:

> Anti-discriminatory practice will work to a model of challenging unfairness. Anti-oppressive practice however works to a model of empowerment and liberation and requires a fundamental re-thinking of values, institutions and relationships. (1992, p. 15)

Phillipson draws attention to the limitations of anti-discriminatory practice because of its legal status:

> legislation against discrimination is fundamentally reformist in orientation, for it is concerned with prompting small scale changes, rather than any fundamental restructuring of power relationships or social values. (1992, pp. 14–15)

Sexual orientation, however, unlike other areas of inequality, has not been afforded the luxury of such small-scale changes; in fact, the opposite is true in that legislation condones discrimination against lesbians and gay men. Given that heterosexuality is not only the dominant ideology but also has legal sanction, it is hard to envisage how social workers can *easily* incorporate in their practice the anti-oppressive perspective outlined above (Logan and Kershaw, 1994).

These developments raise a number of issues for the educators and practitioners who are charged with teaching and assessing students to practise in an anti-discriminatory way. The notion of assessment in anti-discriminatory and anti-oppressive practice is by no means straightforward. The competency model of assessment with its focus on outputs requires students to demonstrate a minimal level or standard of performance. Whilst such a model may be applicable to measuring knowledge and skills, the intangible nature of values mean that they are difficult to measure in terms of outcome.

The CCETSW requirements for beginning practitioners to have a minimum level of competency in anti-discriminatory practice have been interpreted and applied in a broad, all encompassing way. From our experiences as academic tutors and practice teachers, anti-discriminatory practice is generally assessed in relation to race and gender, and sometimes in relation to disability and class.

Rarely, however, is anti-heterosexist practice explicitly considered, either within the academic or practice curriculum. This has been borne out in a recent study of CQSW and in a DipSW practice assessment report which revealed that the vast majority of students and practice teachers failed to address heterosexism or homophobia in their discussions or practice (Trotter and Gilchrist, 1995). A detailed analysis of the few reports which did refer to these issues revealed some reluctance on the part of both social workers and practice teachers to regard the work as central to their anti-oppressive practice agendas.

A number of other themes emerged from the Trotter and Gilchrist report. Firstly, the subject of sexuality arose only if initiated by the clients and there was no routine consideration in supervision, planning, recording or face-to-face work. Secondly, it was only where clients confirmed themselves as being lesbian or gay that these terms were used in the reports; otherwise sexuality could only be guessed at by references to their partner's gender. Thirdly, none of the practice teachers and students who did address lesbian and gay issues in their reports disclosed their own sexuality or its potential relevance to their practice. Finally, and perhaps most significantly, none of the students or practice teachers in any of the 128 reports studied gave any actual examples of anti-heterosexist or non-homophobic practice in their work despite the fact that they are clearly *required* to provide evidence of anti-discriminatory practice. This study confirms that lesbian and gay issues are ignored and that anti-heterosexist practice is overlooked by students and practice teachers. The reasons for this oversight or disregard may be numerous, and are likely to be complex; but denial, as one of the primary manifestations of homophobia, is likely to be a major factor. It is assumed that this denial is located within the practice agency as well as within the college, and is shared by many social work practitioners and educators as well as by students.

Cultural and religious issues

When considering lesbian and gay issues – perhaps more than in any other area of inequality – cultural and religious differences may lead to a fundamental conflict of values for individuals and organisations and set precedents:

> Standpoints supported by religious differences, though also characterised as 'private' are often given greater legitimacy than the professional value base because of their cultural character. (Bremner and Hillin, 1993, p. 56)

This highlights further the complexities involved in promoting anti-oppressive and anti-discriminatory practice, for social work is not concerned with fundamentally changing people's cultural and religious beliefs. What is required is an acceptance of *difference* and an ability to practise in such a way that one's own values are not imposed upon others.

The law

Social workers and probation officers work within a statutory framework which in relation to lesbian and gay issues is both contradictory and confusing. In contrast to other areas of inequality and other oppressed groups, lesbians and gay men are not protected against discrimination by the law; indeed, the opposite is true in that legislation exists which is explicitly discriminatory in nature. The situation is further complicated when considering legislation specific to social work and probation practice which appears to be more flexible and at least recognises the needs of lesbians and gay men. Social workers and probation officers are thus placed in an ambiguous position – on the one hand directed to work in an anti-discriminatory way, yet, on the other operating within a broad legal framework which legitimates discrimination and imposes unfair restrictions (Logan and Kershaw, 1994). This issue will be considered in more detail in Chapter 2.

Equal opportunities policies

Whilst the Race Relations Act (1976) and the Sex Discrimination Act (1975) provide legal mandates in regard to discrimination against women and black people, similar protection has not been given to lesbians and gay men, as there is still an absence of legislation making discrimination on the grounds of sexual orientation illegal. The absence of a parallel legal backing has involved an uphill struggle for the inclusion of sexual orientation in equal opportunities policies. David Waddington, the then Home Office minister, in response to the Labour campaign for lesbian and gay rights, conveyed the extent of the powerful opposition facing them:

> I cannot imagine anything which is more likely to damage the Equal Opportunities Commission than for it to become identified in the public mind with such crankish notions that it would be wrong to discriminate against people on the grounds of homosexuality. (Cited in Evans, 1989/90, p. 76)

Unfortunately, such comments yield much support and continue to do so; and consequently the inclusion of sexual orientation in equal opportunities policies remains patchy.

A research project carried out by the Equal Opportunities Commission in 1990 found that of those probation agencies who replied, 50 per cent refused to include sexual orientation in their equal opportunities policies. Two of the probation agencies in question stated their reasons for doing so: firstly (the committee's) fear of sexual abuse from gay men, and secondly (the committee's) fear of employing gay men in hostels. Such statements are highly discriminatory and directly contravene the guidelines of the National Association of Probation Officers for those working with lesbians and gay men:

> An underlying principle of good Social Work practice is to provide a service based on justice and equality which recognises the real cause of difficulties people face. In order to provide this kind of service to lesbian and gay clients members need to resist the pathologising of a gay or lesbian identity and need to challenge some of their own prejudices and stereotypical attitudes. (NAPO, 1989, p. 1)

Even though authorities now include sexual orientation in their policies, this does not necessarily guarantee the protection of lesbians and gay men, which has been highlighted by the fact that industrial tribunals have rarely upheld or ruled in favour of cases of dis-crimination towards lesbians and gay men (NALGO, 1992).

In relation to social work education, the Association of University Teachers includes sexual orientation in its policy, Cosis Brown never-theless maintains that:

> To come out as a lesbian social work student or teacher still carries risks ... positive developments in social work teaching will not happen until lesbian and gay teachers feel secure in their own institution. (1992, p. 211)

In order to teach students to work in an anti-oppressive way in the general sense, it is important to establish an environment which is safe and supportive. The additional dimensions associated with 'coming out' compound this all the more. The specific issues associated with the invisibility of lesbians and gay men and the notion of 'coming out' will be discussed in more detail in Chapter 3.

2   The legal framework

By comparison with most other European countries, and with much of Australia, Canada and the U.S.A., Britain has more homophobic laws and less legal protection for lesbians and gay people ... Many lesbians and gay men are subjected each year to discrimination, often officially sanctioned in employment, housing, child custody and health care, immigration, local council grants and youth care orders. In total about 20 different points of law either explicitly or by omission discriminate against the lesbian and gay community. The end result is that homosexuals are officially relegated to a second class citizenship, denied equality in law and subject to institutional discrimination in virtually every aspect of our lives. (Tatchell, 1992, p. 237)

The historical context

Before considering the contemporary legal framework, it is relevant to examine the historical context in which sexuality has been socially controlled. Prior to the nineteenth century, homosexuality had not been regarded as a problem (except by the church which regarded sodomy as a punishable sin). The Victorian era, characterised by the growth in industrialisation and capitalism, witnessed the evolution of the patriarchal family unit and the beginning of family ideology. Clearly, anything other than heterosexual relationships would threaten the stability and continuation of the nuclear family hence, as Gittens noted:

The essence of legislation regarding sexuality since the nineteenth century has been concerned with trying to enforce heterosexuality as the only acceptable normal and natural form. (Gittens, 1993, p. 147)

15

Developments in science and medicine subsequently led to the construction of homosexuality as unnatural, pathological and 'sick' and a direct threat to the family unit. The hitherto unchallenged naturalness of the patriarchal family unit would inevitably be threatened by an alternative sexuality which did not fit into the conception of normality and certainly would not ensure its continuation. Thus the nineteenth century witnessed the development of the social construction of homosexuality as a social role (Weeks, 1991) and one which threatened the social and economic structure of society. This deviation theory has remained a constant theme throughout modern capitalist societies. Powerful evidence of this is the fact that homosexuality was considered as mental illness until 1973 in the USA and was illegal in Great Britain until 1967.

The 1967 Sexual Offences Act decriminalised private homosexuality between consenting males over the age of 21. This may seem on the surface to have been a significant step forward in changing attitudes towards homosexuality; however, a more critical analysis suggests only a repressive tolerance (Evans, 1989/90). The message remained that homosexuality was still unacceptable and that the intention of the law had been to control, not to condone.

Despite its limitations, the 1967 act nevertheless encouraged lesbians and gay men into political action during the 1970s. The emergence of Gay Liberation marked the beginnings of the fight for acceptance and was helped by the Women's Movement which also challenged sexual roles and attitudes. Unfortunately legislation passed in the late 1980s represents a heterosexual backlash to the developing liberal attitudes. The emergence of AIDS, conveniently constructed as the Gay Plague, influenced public opinion and fuelled support for the New Right family ideology; and this had a direct effect on legislation (Logan and Kershaw, 1994).

The following overview highlights a complex legal situation. Whilst there are positive elements to some aspects of the law, social workers and probation officers are nonetheless operating within a statutory framework which endorses the discrimination of lesbians and gay men.

The contemporary situation

Section 28

Section 28 of the Local Government Act 1988 states that it is illegal for a local authority to:

a) Intentionally promote homosexuality or publish material with the intention of promoting homosexuality;
b) Promote the teaching ... of the acceptability of homosexuality as a pretended family relationship.

At the point of writing there has been no case law established in respect of Section 28, yet the fear of its contravention has led many local authorities into a position of self-censorship and has resulted in the withholding of funding and service provision. Section 28 has therefore functioned as a powerful moral force, once again sanctioning the primacy of the heterosexual family unit and rendering anything other than this, as inferior and unnatural. The notion of pretended family relationships has permeated other aspects of the law and endorses a government response which is potentially discriminatory.

Fostering and adoption legislation

Section 16 of Consultation Paper No. 16 on fostering in relation to the Children Act 1989 stated that:

> It would be wrong arbitrarily to exclude any particular groups of people from consideration. But the chosen way of life of some adults may mean that they would not be able to provide a suitable environment for the care and nurture of a child ... 'Equal rights' and 'gay rights' policies have no place in fostering services. (DoH, 1990, p. 8).

Whilst the last sentence was subsequently removed, there remains, however, much scope for discrimination against potential lesbian and gay carers whose 'way of life' may be considered unsuitable. The White Paper on adoption (DoH, 1993) reaffirms the government's position that the adoption of children should be the prerogative of married couples only.

Whilst lesbians and gay men can apply to adopt in their own right (i.e. as single applicants), many local authorities remain reluctant to approve or to use lesbian and gay carers for fear of the widespread public and media criticism that this evokes (Hicks, 1993). This practice is despite evidence that children raised by lesbian or gay parents are no more disadvantaged than those raised by heterosexuals (Tasker and Golombok, 1991).

The fostering and adoption of children by lesbians and gay men has, in fact, been going on for a long time, but has usually remained hidden. However, when social services have been able to speak about this fact, they have indicated that lesbian and gay carers made valuable contributions to serving the best interests of children (Skeates and Jabri, 1988).

Age of consent

In comparison to young heterosexual men and women for whom the age of consent for sexual activity is 16, for young gay men the age of consent is 18. Interestingly, young lesbians do not feature in legislation and indeed have never done so. Although in 1921 there was an attempt to make 'gross indecency between female persons' illegal, the bill was not passed in the Lords because they were concerned that legislation would bring the 'horrors of lesbianism to the notice of women who have never heard of it, never thought of it, never dreamed of it' (cited in Gooding, 1992, p. 217).

In 1994, the age of consent for gay men was reduced from 21, as it stood under the Sexual Offences Act 1967, to 18 as part of the Criminal Justice and Public Order Act 1994. Whilst on the surface this may be considered a positive step, it merely serves as a contemporary and salient reminder that homosexuality is not to be considered on an equal basis with heterosexuality.

The legislative background outlined so far is one of clearly mandated discrimination; however, when we turn to legislation specific to social work and probation practice, the outlook is more positive.

The Children Act 1989

For the first time UK legislation refers (in the guidance to the act) to the needs of young people and their sexual identity:

> The needs and concerns of young gay men and women must also be recognised and approached sympathetically. (Sec. 9.50, Vol. 3, Family Placements)

On issues related to young people and counselling, the Act states that:

> Gay men and women may require very sympathetic carers to enable them to accept their sexuality and develop their own self esteem. (Sec. 9.53, Vol. 3, Family Placements)

Given that lesbians and gay men would be well equipped to provide young people with positive self-images, the assertions concerning their unsuitability as carers may deny them the opportunity to provide such a service. Furthermore, the notions of 'pretended family relationships' or the 'promotion of homosexuality' sit uneasily along-side the positive messages contained within the Act, leaving social workers in a dilemma, torn between two opposing mandates. Whilst the 'promotion of homosexuality' is difficult to define and probably more ambiguous than first thought, it nevertheless may be used by some agencies and individual workers as a valid reason for failing to offer an equitable line of service provision, thus denying the needs of some young people (Logan and Kershaw, 1994).

The Criminal Justice Act 1991

For the first time in the law relating to criminal justice, the issue of dis-crimination has been addressed by the inclusion of Section 95 which places an obligation on courts and those agencies involved in the criminal justice system to treat all individuals equally. Section 95 states:

> The Secretary of State shall each year publish such information as he con-siders expedient for the purpose of:

> b) Facilitating the performance by such persons of their duty to avoid dis-criminating against any persons on the grounds of race, sex or any other improper ground. (Sec. 95.1, Criminal Justice Act 1991)

The Probation Service National Standards have explicitly interpreted this section to include sexual orientation. Paradoxically, however, Section 25 of the same Act suggests a re-criminalisation of male homo-sexuality by retaining the definition of gross indecency and soliciting as offences and by the introduction of severe penalties for crimes charged against gay men. This may pose problems for probation offi-cers, not least if they are lesbian or gay themselves and supervising men for what are essentially victimless and consensual offences.

3 Ensuring non-homophobic and anti-heterosexist practice

As indicated earlier, many Diploma in Social Work programmes have failed to address specific lesbian and gay issues within their consideration of anti-discriminatory and anti-oppressive practice. It is relevant then to consider the preparation students are given and the planning that is undertaken by colleges and practice teachers at every stage of the process of teaching and learning, up to and including assessment. The checklist below provides a summary of the preparation and planning required:

- *Pre-course information* To include for prospective students, a statement of values in relation to lesbian and gay issues.
- *Interview and selection* Lesbian and gay perspective to be included by the interviewing panel. Are the questions heterosexist? Questions and responses to be reviewed for evidence of homophobia.
- *Support* Regular support meetings for lesbian and gay students to be held throughout the course which are organised by the programme. Similar support systems need to be made available to students within practice agencies.
- *Consultancy* Lesbian and gay consultants appointed by the programme should be accessible to students during college and placement periods.
- *Academic input* To include lesbian and gay literature and other similar resources throughout the curriculum.
- *Course handbook* All the above information concerning support and consultancy to be included.

A first step in identifying and addressing the issues of non-homophobic and anti-heterosexist practice is to consider the context and framework within which the social work training takes place.

Creating 'safe enough' environments

The initial emphasis must be on creating 'safe enough' environments that will enable students, lecturers and practice teachers to explore the issues. Anti-discriminatory practice, perhaps unlike some other areas of work, is designed to permeate the teaching and learning experience and might reasonably be assessed in all aspects of students' work. The task might well begin within the staff team. Despite (or perhaps in spite of) the equal opportunities policies of various institutions, tutors, lecturers and practice teachers may not have addressed lesbian and gay issues as they apply to day-to-day work, the selection of students or staff development procedures. External assistance and support may be required to raise awareness and reduce the possibility of discriminatory and oppressive practices which may arise in college-based teaching teams or in any team or agency where practice learning takes place.

In order to create an appropriate learning environment, it will be necessary to address issues of both process and content – i.e., not only what is to be taught but also how. Even the comparatively simple action of naming lesbian and gay oppression, or of referring to the possibility of support systems for lesbian or gay students (alongside those for black or women students) may begin to raise consciousness within the student or staff group and may increase the confidence of those wishing to raise these issues.

As with other areas of oppression and discrimination, exploring sexuality can at times be a painful and difficult process. Tutors, students and practice teachers alike need to feel that they can raise questions, gain knowledge and become more confident in their awareness and articulation of the relevant issues. Such a process requires a level of self-appraisal and consideration of the personal impact of viewing oneself as, for example, heterosexual, along with the privileges that this can bestow. This process can only take place in any group within an atmosphere of trust, honesty and clearly negotiated boundaries and expectations.

This can be particularly difficult for students, as there also needs to be a level of shared understanding as to what is to be assessed and how, with clear expectations regarding minimum levels of achievement.

Becoming visible: issues for staff and students

It is particularly relevant within this context to consider the potential difficulties and advantages for lesbian and gay staff and students in deciding to be open about their sexuality. In this sense the question of openness reaches the very heart of the 'invisibility' issues. If these are not addressed, our practice will continue to be both discriminatory and oppressive towards lesbian and gay staff and users of the service.

Whilst we would suggest that such issues must be firmly placed on the agenda for discussion, it is also important to acknowledge that this is a complex area and one about which we do not claim to have all the answers. If nothing else, we hope to raise some of the questions about visibility and invisibility which need to be discussed, re-discussed and discussed again.

Given the heterosexist nature of society, the process a person goes through in deciding that they are lesbian or gay is frequently lengthy and deeply personal as well as sometimes traumatic. Being open about oneself as a lesbian or gay person may be partial or related to particular aspects of one's life, relying on clear 'compartmentalisation' (Davis, 1992) between, for instance, being open with friends but not with colleagues. Clearly this process relies on segregation of different social networks and/or on the explicit or implicit acknowledgement of 'keeping secrets'. The extent to which negative messages and stereotyped images impinge on this process will also reflect the degree to which these are internalised by the individual. Acknowledging our sexuality even to ourselves may bring about celebration or shame, or a mixture of these two conflicting emotions.

For most lesbians and gay men, becoming open about their sexuality is a life-long and gradual process; and the way individuals deal with the effects of heterosexism is part of their personal journey. Consideration about the effect of being open not only relates to possible social isolation but also to the potential loss of home or employment. There are parallels here with other forms of invisible oppression such as that experienced by people with epilepsy, deaf people or those who are HIV positive. It is their invisibleness as well as the lack of legal protection which helps to perpetuate the oppression. This occurs through the process of internalised oppression experienced by the individual and the outward manifestations of homophobia and heterosexism within society as a whole. Consequently a vicious circle is created whereby lesbians and gay men remain fearful of being visible, and therefore the forces which fuel the oppression can remain conveniently unchallenged.

Social work, whilst frequently seen as a liberal and tolerant milieu, also brings together homophobic prejudice, especially in relation to lesbians and gay men working with children or vulnerable adults. First we consider the issues for students and tutors within academic institutions and will return to practice situations later.

The academic environment

To come out as a student or tutor involves risk, as discussed in Chapter 1. The alternative to remaining silent, however, can lead to a double existence shrouded in secrecy and can be equally difficult. It could be reasoned as tactical for staff to reveal their sexuality to students (something which heterosexual colleagues do not of course have to do) and thus challenge heterosexism directly and, some would argue, offer students a positive role model. However, coming out may not receive a positive response, for it cannot be assumed that lesbian and gay students automatically gain support and comfort from lesbian and gay tutors being open about their sexuality. Whilst there is no doubt that this can be the case, anecdotal evidence also suggests that having an openly lesbian or gay tutor is perceived by some lesbian and gay students as a threat to their invisibility and they fear being 'outed' by the process.

Clearly the decision for academic staff to be open about their sexuality will be dependent on a number of factors, not least the support of colleagues. Given that academic institutions reflect wider society, it cannot be taken for granted that the liberal atmosphere generated by so called 'academic freedom', will result in a safe environment. One only has to consider the position of women in an academic world dominated by white middle-class men. Consider then the implications for lesbians, be they black or white! It has been our experience that some heterosexual colleagues challenge the appropriateness of lesbian and gay staff revealing their sexuality, questioning its relevance. Indeed, the issue of appropriateness is significant, but only in so far as deciding when and how to come out rather than whether to come out or not. When teaching about issues of sexuality, the decision to be open or not becomes poignant. Some would argue that not to come out in these circumstances is colluding with the very oppression which is being challenged. Robinson holds the view that lecturers should be open about their sexuality:

> in classes which are charged with vulnerability, passionate emotion and sometimes personal revelations, I feel it is important for an honest dialogue to occur (say when a lesbian student comes out in class), that I

should respond with a similar level of openness, whilst recognising power imbalances between us. (Robinson, 1993, p. 80)

Keating proposes a different strategy, however, and argues that the uncertainty and ambiguity caused by not revealing one's sexuality might more effectively challenge students' expectations or assumptions.

By engaging in what I call 'strategic nonnaming'. That is, I make a point of not identifying as heterosexual, bisexual, or lesbian. (Keating, 1994, p. 98)

A recent comment by a student to a lecturer who had come out during a teaching session illustrates further the implications of disclosure:

I think you're brave for what you did but I'd never come out because I'd become known as Sue the lesbian rather than just Sue.

This leads to a further consideration for lesbian and gay staff and students in deciding whether to be visible – that is, the risk of being seen as the 'expert' on lesbian and gay issues, thereby exonerating other (heterosexual) colleagues from tackling the lesbian and gay agenda. This is of course an issue faced by all oppressed groups. Black or disabled staff, for instance, frequently face the experience of being placed in the role of expert and guardian of good practice in relation to anti-racism and anti-disablism; of course there is no question of whether to be open or not in order to expect more from white and/or non-disabled colleagues.

Support within the academic environment

The issue of support for lesbian and gay students within programmes can be seen as crucial, yet is in danger of being clouded or ignored because of the visible/invisible dichotomy. It has been our experience that until students openly say that they are gay or lesbian, the issue of support is rarely addressed. It is, however, up to programme providers to lead the way and to be proactive.

It is not enough to say that most, if not all, universities and colleges through the student's union, provide gay, lesbian and bisexual support groups. In many cases these exist in an informal way and organise social events for students across all departments. In addition, the programme provider should also facilitate opportunities for gay and lesbian social work students to meet to discuss the particular problems they may face during the course and in practice placements. It is essential that this process begins prior to the start of the course.

The practice learning environment

Whilst there are common issues concerning the decision of lesbians and gay men to be open about their sexuality irrespective of the context, some areas of social work practice carry more risks for the individual than others. As acknowledged earlier, workers within the child-care field will be more exposed to the sharp edge of homophobia. Despite the fact that sexual abuse of children is mainly perpetrated by heterosexual men (Finkelhor, 1986; Campbell, 1988), the view that gay men in particular have a tendency towards paedophilia is still widely, albeit erroneously, held. This view was not helped by the recent allegations widely reported in the press about a professional who held senior and influential roles within social work, who had a long history of being involved in the sexual abuse of children – a predilection which he attempted, and indeed succeeded for many years, to cover up by falsely assuming a gay identity.

Within the social work profession, however, there is a responsibility to draw on relevant research and knowledge which appropriately informs our practice in all areas of oppression. It could be argued that if social work organisations were more informed about lesbian and gay lifestyles, then the opportunity for paedophiles to forge deception through this avenue would be reduced.

Within group care settings where the boundaries between the personal and the professional are less clearly defined, lesbians and gay men may feel even more vulnerable. The level of contact between worker and client is not only greater but more intense, both emotionally and physically. The decision to be open as a lesbian or gay man can be more acute, whilst hiding one's sexuality is a precarious business. In group care settings, questions about a worker's personal life are commonplace; unlike lesbian and gay men, heterosexual staff do not usually have to consider whether or not they should tell a young person that they are in a relationship. This is a complex and sensitive debate which, whilst beyond the remit of this publication, is worthy of further attention.

Would it be appropriate to disclose one's sexuality in a situation where a young person comes out to a member of staff or to a student who is lesbian or gay. There is no correct answer to the question, but what is important is that all staff are supportive to the young person concerned, as confirmed by the following testimony:

> what would have been useful was someone who was sensitive and sympathetic and trustworthy to talk to – it would not need to be a gay person. Information about where you could get confidential advice and support,

or about local gay groups, would have made a big difference. (*Community Care*, 2–8 March, 1995, p. 23)

Support in relation to practice learning

For a number of reasons, it is vitally important that lesbian and gay staff and students feel safe about being open regarding their sexuality with their colleagues, because the social work task is demanding enough without the added stress of fearing that they may be exposed. Clearly if 'safe enough' environments are created for staff, then every-one gains including service users.

In group care settings the particular emphasis on team work is crucial to good practice. Staff rely heavily on one another and there-fore support is central to the team. Lesbian and gay colleagues need to feel as supported as anyone else, whether or not this is due to a personal or professional joy or crisis. The fact of their sexuality should not be a source of loose talk or gossip.

Safe environments have to be created for staff and students where some of these negative attitudes and consequences can be reduced. Without this security, lesbian and gay students are seriously dis-advantaged and unable to learn by honestly confronting the common-alities and differences in their relationships with practice teachers and colleagues.

It is important for agencies to work within a clearly stated equal opportunities framework that applies to service users and staff and covers all areas where discrimination is unacceptable, including that against lesbians and gay men. In addition, practice learning agencies should develop a code of practice which enables lesbian and gay students to make choices about being 'out'. Such a decision should be based on personal circumstances rather than concern as to their 'safety', acceptability and the assessment of their professional compe-tence.

Students need to be reassured that being lesbian or gay will not be a factor in the way work is allocated or transferred and that they will receive the full support of the department in the event of being chal-lenged by service users in relation to being lesbian or gay. In addition, they need reassurance about not being seen as experts or the only ones to challenge homophobia or heterosexism.

Practice teacher training and assessment

Before practice teachers can assist students in their development of anti-discriminatory practice, it is essential that they are adequately trained themselves. Many practice teachers completed their training as social workers before anti-oppressive practice became a core element of training; consequently the whole concept of anti-oppressive practice, particularly as it relates to lesbians and gay men, may be a new consideration for some. Their sensitivity to lesbian and gay colleagues or service users may not be developed, and their lack of awareness of homophobia and heterosexism may cause them to overlook poor practice or fail to give credit for competent practice. It is possible that such 'inexpertise' may result in incorrect appraisal, especially when assessing a gay or lesbian student who may be working appropriately with discriminatory or oppressive clients, colleagues, agencies or supervisors.

CCETSW now recommends that practice teachers be accredited, involving an assessment of their competence and the provision of evidence in relation to anti-discriminatory and anti-oppressive practice. Practice teachers must:

> Demonstrate and integrate social work values into all aspects of practice teaching ... Recognise, challenge and act against racism and discrimination. (CCETSW, 1995b, p. 13)

As part of this process, practice teachers are required to submit a portfolio of material to an assessment board. Candidates are provided with guidelines intended to help them prepare for their submission. Rarely, however, do such guidelines explicitly address anti-heterosexist practice.

Practice teacher training programmes require candidates to demonstrate how they address issues of anti-racist practice with students, and this must be included in the submitted portfolio along with examples of teaching anti-oppressive practice from other areas of oppression. As already mentioned, evidence suggests that this is one area of oppression which most practice teachers would rarely choose to address (Trotter and Gilchrist, 1995).

In order to promote anti-heterosexist practice, it is essential that gay and lesbian issues are overtly addressed by all practice teachers irrespective of their sexuality, and this should be made explicit to all candidates who wish to attain the CCETSW Practice Teaching Award. In order to achieve this, all practice teacher training and assessment programmes need to examine their procedures and teaching input to address the invisibility of lesbian and gay issues. This would result in fairer assessment for lesbian and gay practice teachers who may be unfairly judged by examiners whose own lack of awareness or even homophobia could be detrimental to the candidate(s). It is therefore the responsibility of the programmes to provide explicit guidelines which actively include a lesbian and gay perspective on their training courses and assessment boards, as set out in the checklist below:

Practice teacher training

- Inclusion of lesbian and gay issues in the training programme.
- Use of lesbian and gay practitioners in the delivery of teaching and the assessment process whenever possible.

Assessment of practice teachers

- Guidelines on preparing the portfolio to explicitly include the need for practice teachers to address lesbian and gay issues.
- Programmes may want to consider a similar provision of consultancy for lesbian and gay students as already exists for black students. Consultants could work on behalf of the assessment board and ensure the provision of a lesbian and gay perspective as well as providing support for students when necessary.
- Appeals procedures to state clearly the process involved if candidates feel homophobia has unfairly influenced the final assessment of their portfolio.

4 Teaching and learning strategies

Introduction

> Competence in social work is the product of knowledge, skills and values ... students will have to demonstrate that they have: met practice requirements; integrated social work values; acquired and applied knowledge; reflect upon and critically analyzed their practice; and transferred knowledge, skills and values in practice. (CCETSW, 1995a, p. 17)

The aim of both academic and practice teaching in relation to lesbian and gay issues is to enable students to develop their awareness and understanding of oppression, to unlearn heterosexist assumptions and to develop strategies for challenging heterosexist or homophobic attitudes and practices. Students therefore need knowledge of:

- Theories of oppression, disadvantage and discrimination and their impact at a structural and individual level, including an understanding of the correlation between various forms of oppression.
- Historical perspectives as they affect lesbians and gay men, including a critical analysis of how sexuality has been socially constructed over time.
- Legislation and equal opportunities policies as they affect lesbians and gay men.

Programmes must also be designed to ensure that lesbian and gay perspectives permeate the curriculum generally, and students should be encouraged to adopt a critical approach to their learning. For example, lesbian and gay perspectives should be incorporated into the following areas of study: models of human growth and develop-

31

ment; concepts of normality and difference; the nature of the family; the impact of loss, transition and change.

Students should also be provided with opportunities to explore their own personal values and attitudes in relation to lesbian and gay sexuality. This should incorporate a recognition of diversity and difference within a multi-racial, multi-cultural and multi-faith Britain and the potential for conflict between organisational, professional and individual values.

Following on from this, students should be encouraged to critically analyse traditional social work literature and should be provided with lesbian and gay literature and resources. It is important that materials reflect the range and diversity of lifestyles, including other aspects of oppression in order to avoid the stereotypes of lesbians and gay men being young, white and non-disabled. Materials and exercises for use in both the academic and practice learning environments are in 'Teaching/Training Material' on pages 57–104.

In addition students should have opportunities to critically analyse their practice in relation both to their own knowledge and values and to all aspects of the social work process from initial contact through assessment and intervention. Phillipson has written about the necessity of adopting a 'gendered' lens in relation to practice; it is also important to have a similar lens in relation to sexuality.

The framework developed by Phillipson presented in Figure 4.1 is particularly helpful for students to conceptualise the links between knowledge and the skills of anti-oppressive practice within the social work process.

This framework can be applied in a variety of ways: for example, with a student working in a situation involving a black gay man seeking respite care for his 15-year-old son who has learning disabilities. Figure 4.2 shows how the framework can be applied.

Preparation for teaching/training

Before turning to the 'Teaching/Training Material' on pages 57–104, there are a number of important issues to be considered, as covered in the following section. As a starting point, it is important when planning sessions to be clear about the aims and objectives, as the needs of Diploma in Social Work students may be markedly different from those of practice teachers and agency managers.

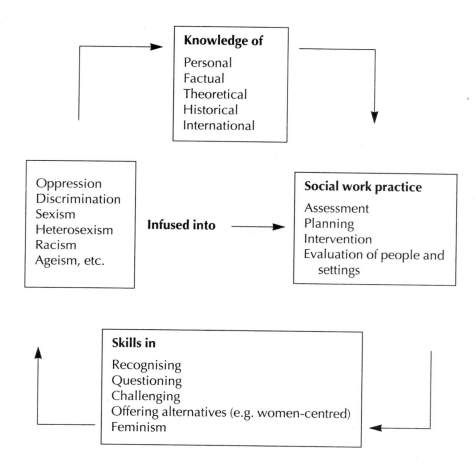

Figure 4.1   The links between knowledge and skills
Source: J. Phillipson, 1992, p. 40

Self-preparation

> Because human sexuality is so intensely personal, any change in attitudes towards homosexuality must begin on a personal level. The first step in this process rests with the social workers, who must begin to examine their attitudes towards homosexuality. (Gramich, 1988, p. 140)

As Gramich points out, the starting point has to be with oneself, and this applies to educators, to practice teachers and to students. Before exploring matters of sexuality with the students, it is essential that

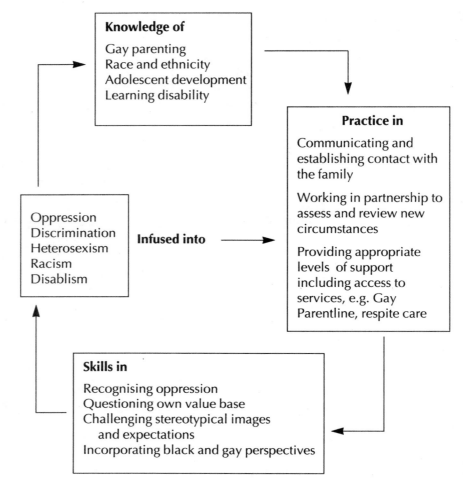

Figure 4.2   Applying the framework

educators and practice teachers address 'where they are coming from' in relation to their own sexuality and deal with any issues arising from this. If they have not already done so, they should participate in a course covering lesbian and gay sexuality. At the very least, educators and practice teachers should take part in the exercises presented in this book before using them with students.

Further awareness and understanding can be gained by accessing lesbian and gay history and culture through films, books, theatre and art. Not only would this provide a rich and diverse source of interest and knowledge, but also it would help to counterbalance the often negative view of lesbian and gay lifestyles.

The learning environment

Sexuality exposes our human frailty and vulnerability as well as our strengths; it also continues to be a taboo subject. For this reason, it remains one of the most demanding and challenging areas of social work practice and education. Add to this the prejudice and fear that fuel homophobia, and we begin to understand why lesbian and gay sexuality (or indeed sexuality in general) is seldom adequately addressed.

Any course which touches upon personal and emotive issues, and in particular those which challenge prejudice and discrimination, may feel threatening or distressing. The invisibility of sexuality and for some the long-held cultural and religious beliefs compound these issues all the more. Every student has a contribution to make based on life experiences and knowledge, but in order to feel safe and to share and learn from one another, an environment conducive to learning has to be created.

Any group of whatever size will include individuals from a wide diversity of backgrounds and life experiences. Some will be lesbian or gay and may be open about their sexuality. Those who are not 'out' may fear being exposed and may find it difficult to join in discussions, whereas those who are 'out' may be concerned about being the focus of attention or regarded as experts. Some students may never have been in a situation where sexuality has been discussed and may find it embarrassing to participate, while others may have strongly held opinions which they are able to articulate. When considering issues of safety, we must constantly ask 'safety for whom'? Whilst an environment which allows people to make mistakes is crucial, we must be aware that one person's safety could result in another person's vulnerability.

Allowing sufficient time to create a safe, supportive atmosphere at the beginning of a course session will largely determine the success or failure of the session; and establishing working agreements and ground rules are essential to this process. Each group will need to negotiate its own framework, and every group member has to take some responsibility in this.

Outlined below are some specific factors to note in regard to the learning environment.

Training venue

The venue should be accessible for disabled people and be well equipped to meet individual needs. The room should be large enough to comfortably accommodate students, allowing them space to move around and form small groups if and when required. Keeping people together in one room, even when split into subgroups, enables the teacher/trainer to monitor individual group processes and progress.

Group size

Particularly when inviting students to discuss personal issues, determining the size of the group is very important. Too large a group can often result in the more confident and vocal student dominating the discussions, whilst others feel overshadowed, frustrated or inadequate and thus unable to contribute. This suggests that each group should perhaps be limited to between four and six people in order to encourage maximum participation.

The facilitator(s)

If the group is fairly small, most of the exercises in Part 2 can be facilitated by one person. However, many courses carry large numbers of students, making it difficult to manage subjects which touch upon personal issues. Whenever possible, it is useful to consider both female and male presenters working together and to involve both heterosexual and lesbian and gay teachers/trainers. Clearly a broad range of perspectives will bring added depth and meaning to the teaching.

A safety warning

Students should be made aware that when asked to consider personal issues, this may trigger past or current experiences for them. Consequently, teachers/trainers should feel confident in handling such matters and be able to encourage student awareness about the level at which they approach the subject matter.

Effective learning

It is important to take into account strategies for effective teaching and learning (Kolb et al., 1974) as well as individual learning styles (Honey and Mumford, 1986). When planning a programme, exercises should be carefully selected so that they not only address the objectives of the programme, but also utilise a variety of exercises and activities in order to make the teaching effective and to maximise students' learning.

Format of session

Sessions should include formal lecture inputs (which could be adapted from Chapters 1 and 2 in this book) followed by a selection of exercises presented in Part 2 – all of which offer a degree of student participation and thus the opportunity of learning by doing – a successful method of acquiring knowledge and skills. Video clips can be used as supplements to the training and are valuable in providing an added visual dimension and can often convey a wealth of information in a relatively short space of time (see Part 2).

The suggested timetables in Figures 4.3 and 4.4 give some useful ideas in providing a format for the learning environment.

Programme 1	**Raising awareness**
1.00 pm	Introduction to the course
1.05 pm	Ice breaker
1.20 pm	Working agreement
1.35 pm	Sexual messages
2.05 pm	Feedback
2.15 pm	Break
2.30 pm	Myths exercise and feedback
3.15 pm	Lifestyles and prejudice exercise
4.15 pm	Closing circle
4.30 pm	Finish

Figure 4.3　Sample timetable

Programme 2	Raising awareness and practice issues
9.30 am	Introduction
9.35 am	Ice breaker
9.45 am	Working agreement
10.00 am	Lecture
10.30 am	Sexuality quiz/discussion
11.00 am	Break
11.15 am	'Your move' exercise/discussion
12.15 pm	Group exercise
1.00 pm	Lunch
2.00 pm	Recap from the morning session
2.15 pm	Lecture: Social work practice with lesbians and gay men
3.00 pm	Group exercise – The Law and Oppression/feedback
3.15 pm	Break
3.00 pm	Case study
4.15 pm	Action planning
4.25 pm	Course evaluation
4.30 pm	Finish

Figure 4.4   Sample timetable

Practice learning opportunities

A core element of practice teaching is to 'manage the integration of the student's learning needs' (CCETSW, 1995b). Within the context of anti-oppressive practice, it is essential that students are given the opportunity to consider *all* oppressed groups. In relation to anti-heterosexist practice this should not be narrowly interpreted as an opportunity for working directly with lesbian or gay service users.

Such an approach would be highly inappropriate, for anti-heterosexist practice is important work with all service users (a parallel here is when addressing issues of race). Given the invisibility of lesbians and gay men, it is indeed possible that students may be working unknowingly with service users who are lesbian or gay. It is therefore essential that students are assessed in terms of their own values, attitudes, assumptions and interventions throughout all aspects of the social work process. The onus is therefore on the practice teacher to provide the students with the relevant opportunity to address the issues, test their value base and develop their skills in this area. This process might be what Audre Lorde refers to as 'the transformation of silence into language and action' (cited in Garber, 1994, p. 96).

The issue of the invisibility of lesbians and gay men presents a particular challenge to practice teachers and students, as self-determination and confidentiality are central themes in working with lesbian and gay service users and may lead students and practice teachers to underestimate the volume of evidence they can present for assessment. While there is a need to respect an individual's right not to be open about their sexuality, students, nevertheless, have to be given the opportunity to address their values and practice in this area.

In order to do this, practice teachers need to alert students to potential lesbian and gay issues early on in their work with service users. Students should also have the opportunity to explore their own values and attitudes in relation to sexuality. In addition, appropriate reading/resources/information should be made available. In further practice teaching sessions students will require adequate time to review their integration of these issues in practice. An example of this process is described below:

> A student on placement in a residential child-care setting was approached by a young woman who told him that other girls at a disco said she looked like a man because of her style of dress. While she was with the student, she noticed information leaflets on local lesbian and gay organisations which he suggested she take away to read. This student had already been alerted to issues of sexuality in working with young people, and had been encouraged to explore his own values and attitudes as a white heterosexual man .
>
> . His practice teacher suggested some specific reading (Bremner and Hillin, 1993; Winterson, 1987) and the student was able to attend a workshop on lesbian and gay issues in social work. In supervision he was encouraged to rehearse possible ways of interviewing and supporting the young woman concerned, recognising her right to control the pace of the work and her choice of him as a worker.

If there are no occasions to address the issues discussed in the example above, learning opportunities could be provided in a number of different ways – for example, within the practice teaching session, case scenarios can be used to stimulate discussion with students about the relevant issues involved. Other learning situations are outlined below.

What if?

In presenting a 'live' case, students can be asked 'what if the user of the service was lesbian or gay'? This approach can also raise issues about 'presumed' heterosexuality and its affect on lesbians and gay men.

A 'what if' can be further developed by adding other dimensions such as disability, race, culture, religion etc. So, for instance, a student could be asked what the issues would be for a disabled lesbian, thus bringing disability and gender into focus as well. This process helps address issues around the experience of multi-oppression and provides the opportunity for the student to deepen and strengthen his/her knowledge, skills and value base.

Recording and report writing

This is a key area for students to demonstrate competence in gathering appropriate and relevant information and recording it coherently within a non-judgemental framework. To help with this process students could be asked to critically assess a series of reports or case recordings, with particular reference to their value base. Due to the invisibility issue for lesbians and gay men, practice teachers may have to use invented reports which test the students' ability to pick out heterosexism.

Group care settings

The very nature of group care settings means that practice is generally more visible. However, for lesbians and gay men (whether service users, staff or students) their invisibility may be even more acute. To be open about their sexuality (either by choice or lack of it) within a living environment will involve a whole set of possible consequences, from which there may be no respite or refuge. The need to address issues of safety is particularly pertinent. Practice teachers working in group care settings can use the methods referred to above; in addition, the following suggestions may be of value.

Ask students to talk through a typical 24-hour-period within the life of the residential home or day centre; paying particular attention to heterosexism. This may be implicit – i.e., 'presumed heterosexuality' of everyone – or explicit in terms of derogatory remarks or behaviour towards and about lesbians and gay men. Heterosexism may also manifest itself in the books, films, TV programmes etc. chosen by the residents and staff.

This process will heighten students' awareness of the existence of heterosexism within daily life. From here they could be asked to discuss strategies for appropriately challenging heterosexism within the home or centre.

Students should not be left to feel responsible for the level of heterosexism that may exist within their placement. On the positive side, if heterosexism is already being addressed within the home or centre, students could be asked to discuss how this might be further developed.

Those working in group care settings may also find the models of good practice outlined in Chapters 5 and 6 helpful.

Indirect practice

We have talked about the issues of invisibility and the need to respect an individual's choice not to be open about their sexuality. Schoenberg and Goldberg (1984) suggest indirect practice – for example, administration, resource appraisal and development, policy development, lobbying and community organisation – as areas where students can demonstrate their skills without compromising principles of confidentiality.

Checklists

As part of a practice teaching session students could be asked to provide a checklist, indicating good practice within a number of different social work settings. The models of good practice already discussed may again be helpful in this process. Such an approach could be developed further by asking students to identify the issues and how they could assist lesbians or gay men who wished to be open about their sexuality.

5 Assessment

Introduction

Students must be assessed for their understanding of knowledge and theory, and their ability to integrate values in practice. However, as mentioned in Chapter 1, whilst a competency model of assessment may be applicable to measuring knowledge and skills, the assessment of values is more complex and has provoked considerable debate (Jordan et al., 1993; Gilchrist and Trotter, 1996). Hager et al. (1994) noted that attitudes and values are so difficult to assess that they might as well be 'left out' of the competency based approach to assessment. However, these authors suggest that the difficulties are more aligned to abstract ideas which become less difficult when applied to practice. They argue that other researchers (notably Gonczi et al., 1993) have found professional opinions to be reliable and consistent in their assessments; the use of performance criteria in the competencies increases professionals' reliability and their expertise sensitises them to greater accuracy in assessment. There are, however, a number of difficulties with these arguments when relating to the assessment of anti-oppressive practice and anti-heterosexist practice in particular. Clearly this is a complex area, whilst the aim of this book is to provide positive and practical ways forward.

CCETSW (1995a, p.23) specifically requires students to demonstrate an awareness of 'Sources and forms of oppression, disadvantage and discrimination based on: race, gender, religion, age, class, being gay and lesbian, and disability, and their impact at a structural and individual level.' Being gay and lesbian is thus identified as a specific source of oppression which students are required to address and which practice teachers are required to assess.

43

Knowledge and awareness of homophobia and heterosexism, and non-homophobic and anti-heterosexist practice may all need to be assessed in different ways and at different stages. It is, however, essential that students are clear about what they are being assessed for and how they are being assessed.

Academic assessment

There are a variety of ways in which a student's academic learning can be assessed including traditional essay writing, project work, report style assignments, etc. Whatever method is adopted, it is important that students are informed of the assessment criteria before they begin working on the assignment and receive detailed feedback in relation to the criteria.

Marking criteria are now frequently given to students, and although these vary considerably in their purpose and value, they can be used specifically to assign marks to anti-discriminatory and anti-oppressive practice. Anonymous marking is also being increasingly used by some programmes, although success in terms of grades relating to 'majority/minority' groups has yet to be proven in relation to lesbian and gay students. Clearly, in terms of practice assessment, anonymity is not appropriate, and students' sexuality as well as their race, gender, etc. may be crucial elements in their practice.

The following checklist may be useful in ensuring that lesbian and gay issues are addressed within programmes:

- Set an agreed definition of what constitutes anti-discriminatory/anti-oppressive practice for staff, students and practice teachers.
- Set consistent criteria for the students to be measured against.
- Set agreed areas/types of discrimination/oppression to focus on, and state minimum expected.
- Set specific marking criteria for anti-discriminatory practice in all assignments.
- Set minimum levels of achievement expected for years one and two.
- Ensure that anti-discriminatory practice is an essential element in all assignment titles or exam questions.
- Include anti-heterosexist and non-homophobic issues in the feedback given to students.

Practice assessment

> It is only practice which is founded on values, carried out in a skilled manner and informed by knowledge, critical analysis and reflection which is complete practice. (CCETSW, 1995b, p. 3)

Whilst the aim of teaching students about lesbian and gay oppression is to increase their knowledge and awareness, this does not necessarily guarantee their ability to translate their increased understanding into practice. Richards has suggested that awareness is only the beginning:

> For the confident, intelligent and energetic learner this is often the natural precursor to focused planning and imaginative intervention. For others, the sheer complexity opened up can lead to muddled thinking or ineffectual stereotypical reactions whose validity or reliability are never scrutinised. (Richards, 1988, p. 9)

In relation to the process of assessment, it is therefore important that students are assisted to translate their increased awareness into action, as suggested in Chapter 4. This is crucial for the task of the practice teacher which, as outlined by CCETSW (1995b, p. 3), should be to: 'Seek *evidence* of the integration of knowledge and values in students' practice'.

In relation to practice therefore, students should be demonstrating that they are using current knowledge and research findings to inform every aspect of their work. In addition, they should be identifying and challenging heterosexist assumptions in reports, recording, referrals, etc. – indeed, in any aspect of the social work process. For example, in regard to fostering and adoption, students should be demonstrating evidence of their own views about lesbian and gay parenting, incorporating current research findings into their practice and using research to challenge assumptions and myths about lesbians and gay men.

It is perhaps important to remember that the aim of social work education is not to *change* students values *per se*; the essence is to value diversity and difference. Students must therefore demonstrate an awareness of their own values and an awareness of what they do with them!

The debate about how one effectively assesses values will no doubt continue and rightly so. In the meantime it is important that those involved in the assessment process do not feel immobilised either by the complexity or the tensions inherent in the task. In a sense the assessment of values within practice teaching can only be advanced by continuing to refine and adapt the process. Assignments and study assessment criteria need to be continually analysed and reviewed. As awareness and familiarity with the issue grows and develops, so will the ability to provide more sophisticated assessment criteria.

6 A model of good practice

Broad statements about anti-oppressive practice in relation to sexuality are meaningless unless they translate into tangible action. One way forward is to provide students in Diploma in Social Work programmes with a good practice guide or 'ideal-type' to help them unpick the complexities of the issues involved and assess the quality of the service being provided to lesbians and gay men.

The starting place for such a model should come from the central power base of the organisation and permeate through every level. Only then can the foundations be created for positive developments at the operational level of the team.

Departmental policies

As already indicated, legislation is rarely helpful in this arena, as it keeps lesbians invisible and criminalises the behaviour of gay men, particularly those under the age of 18. Departmental policies are usually shaped and formed by legislation. Within particular aspects of lesbian and gay sexuality, however, a tension exists between the law, the prejudice that envelops it, and the philosophy of anti-oppressive practice. Examples of this can be found among the following groups: gay men under 18, lesbian mothers fighting for custody of their children, lesbian and gay foster carers and learning disabled people. At a senior level within both voluntary and statutory organisations, this tension has to be addressed and a clear lead given on anti-oppressive practice. Policies which support and maintain a sound anti-oppressive and anti-discriminatory philosophy need to be formulated and resourced in order to provide the corner stone for developing practice. Some suggested policies are discussed below.

Equal opportunities policies

Equal opportunities policies must be clear in their directive to staff and users that the aim of the organisation is to deliver a service free from discrimination. The use of appropriate language is crucial: if social work organisations are serious in their intent to protect and promote the rights of lesbian and gay staff and service users, then the language used must reflect this. Terms such as 'sexuality', 'sexual orientation' or 'sexual preference' are either vague, unclear or dangerously misleading. Do social work organisations really welcome applications from people whose sexual preference is towards children? Clearly such a suggestion is absurd; but unless the language is precise, it leaves lesbians and gay men exposed to absurdity, ambiguity and continued mythology about their lifestyles.

The use of the words 'lesbian' and 'gay' is the acceptable language that organisations should adopt. This is not only the chosen terminology of many lesbians and gay men but is also the language which suggests a lifestyle rather than a preoccupation with sex, thereby dispelling another homophobic myth. The use of 'lesbian' and 'gay' also signals a clear message that the organisation is serious in its support of lesbian and gay staff and service users.

A sense of ownership of the policy by all employees and service users is central to its being effective. To achieve this, staff and users must be involved in developing and launching (or reviewing) equal opportunities policies. Consultations, monitoring exercises, training sessions and discussion groups should be facilitated, publicised and resourced; and time allocated to allow all staff to attend, contribute to, and learn from the process.

Implementation of the policy requires continued involvement from all levels of the organisation. One way this might be achieved is the establishment of a task group which could undertake a range of activities, some of which are detailed below. Membership of the group would include representatives from all sections and levels of the organisations with the responsibility for developing, maintaining, monitoring and evaluating the policy and procedures.

Training and development

Staff throughout the organisation require training to be able to implement departmental policies in relation to equal opportunities and to develop their anti-oppressive practice. Whilst some groups of staff may require training specifically tailored to meet their needs, a broad-based approach could offer most staff the opportunity to review their practice and procedures with regard to heterosexism and homophobia.

Maintenance strategies

Strategies for maintaining the equal opportunities policy should be established at different points within the organisation. Complaints procedures must be accessible for users of the service; grievance procedures accessible for staff, and disciplinary procedures should give access to the organisation. These procedures should be used whenever breaches of the equal opportunities policy have been identified.

Staff and users of the service need to be aware of the range of procedures to which they have recourse and of how each process operates. Staff with specific responsibility, i.e. managers, for implementing such procedures, also require training which should include awareness of the oppression and discrimination, of all disadvantaged groups.

Monitoring and evaluation

The role of the task group in relation to monitoring and evaluation should be to set a base-line. This could be done by devising a questionnaire for all work units requesting detailed information on how the policy translates into practice. Examples of questions might include:

- How is your work place challenging heterosexism?
- What anti-racist strategies do you have in place?
- How accessible is your building?
- How are you supporting lesbian and gay staff and users?
- What are the training needs of your staff in regard to anti-oppressive practice?

Such an approach has to be seen as supportive and at the same time clear that the issues are serious and will not be avoided – for example, by locating this work in the standards and quality assurance department. There should be an understanding that individuals and teams will be at different stages in their awareness and ability to respond. In assisting the task group in their development of sound practice, trainers and appropriate materials must be available as well as other resources such as books, posters, films, advice and information centres.

Models of supervision and support

Crucial to good practice is the availability of appropriate support and supervision. Staff must be able to explore their own feelings in relation to sexuality and how these impact on their work. Lesbian and gay staff need to explore how homophobia affects them as well as their service users. All staff need to be able to explore positive strategies for responding.

Good models of support and supervision need to be owned from the centre of the organisation. In this way, acceptable base-line standards are set across the organisation as a whole, rather than the more familiar situation of pockets of good support and supervision programmes amidst poor or non-existent ones. It is not enough for employers or line managers to focus only on helping alleviate problems on an individual basis for lesbian and gay staff. They should take a proactive lead in challenging and changing the work environment through the supervision and support offered to all staff.

Training which provides effective models of supervision and support should be available to all staff who have supervisory responsibility. There is also an established body of literature addressing supervision which should be made available (Hawkins and Shohet, 1989).

Sexual health education

In residential, day care and fostering situations, there is a specific need for staff to be guided by clear, safe and supportive policies regarding sexual health education. Such policies should take account of lesbian and gay lifestyles in a positive and proactive manner – for example, policies should *not* only address issues of sexuality in a context of HIV/AIDS. It is important to remember also that colleagues can be a vital resource in terms of their knowledge base and experience. In addition, there are a number of training packs, books and other materials available on this subject (see Aggleton et al., 1990; CCETSW, 1993).

Selection and recruitment

A clearly defined policy on selection and recruitment, consistent with equal opportunities, and owned by the department as a whole is necessary to carry forward an anti-oppressive philosophy.

The departmental policy should reflect a non-judgemental attitude towards user groups, especially those already disadvantaged by their position in society, even though there will be specific guidelines relating to particular user groups (i.e. police checks for candidates applying to work with children and young people). Selection processes must test non-judgemental attitudes irrespective of the post applied for, and avoid being mechanistic. Selection and recruitment policies must therefore develop over time and reflect the rich diversity in the organisation, which depends on carefully targeted publicity.

Training of staff with responsibility for recruitment (including selection of volunteers) is a central component and one essential to the process. Similarly, training and preparation is also needed when involving service users in the selection process.

A sample programme for a two-day selection interview is provided in Figure 6.1 which can be adapted to suit different settings.

Day 1	
2.00 pm	Arrival of candidates – tea/coffee Introductions Information about the agency Outline agency process of interview
2.30 pm	Written exercise to identify value base in a particular situation
3.15 pm	Coffee/tea
3.45 pm	Candidates' group discussion on specified topic (observed – group skills, knowledge base, value base)
4.30 pm	Break
5.00 pm	Service users interview panel
6.00 pm	Candidates depart – asked to phone in to confirm shortlisting
Day 2	(shortlisted candidates)
2.00 pm	Brief observed role play – staff member and candidate
2.45 pm	Tea/coffee
3.00 pm	Final staff panel interview

Figure 6.1   Programme for a selection interview

Information from each stage of the processes outlined should be fed into the final staff panel interview.

A team approach

A team approach to positively address issues for lesbians and gay men should occur more easily by adopting the policies outlined above and by referring to the checklist below:

- How are staff selected?
- What is the user involvement in this process?
- How do users view their involvement?
- How easy would it be for a user of the service to 'come out'?
- How easy would it be for a worker to 'come out'?
- What is the philosophy of the team and how is this communicated?
- How diverse is the team?
- What does the physical environment convey?
- What are the supervision and support programmes in place?
- What are team meetings like?
- How safe does it feel to disagree?
- Are different views heard and respected?

To expand on the checklist, the following discussion illustrates the crucial role that teams play in ensuring good practice.

Selection and recruitment

Each team has its own particular requirements in relation to staffing. Within a clear framework, as outlined above, it is more likely that these will be adequately addressed, and appropriate appointments made.

The importance of user involvement was referred to in the last section. It is at the team or section level that the fundamentals of this involvement become realised, ensuring service user needs do not become marginalised.

Diversity of teams

Service users are a diverse group of people, and staff teams need to reflect this (Mills, 1995). Such diversity is crucial in conveying the message that 'difference' is something to celebrate. As mentioned earlier, it is particularly important to ensure that job adverts reach as wide a circulation as possible.

Supervision and support

From the basis of a clear departmental policy, supervision pro-grammes can be developed which are appropriate to the particular setting. In many instances, a group supervision model can be devel-oped, not in place of individual supervision but complementary to it. Group supervision allows for exploration of group dynamics of both the user group and the staff team and provides a forum for under-standing how one affects the other. It also provides a forum for the development of innovative practice from the team as a whole. Most importantly, within the consideration of lesbian and gay issues, group supervision allows for the awareness and understanding to be developed on a group as well as an individual basis.

Physical environment

The physical environment of the workplace (or living space for users of residential establishments) is crucial in the endorsement of poli-cies and in sustaining good practice. Messages about the service pro-vided are conveyed graphically and powerfully by the appearance of reception areas, offices, living spaces, storage rooms and even the exterior of the premises. Pictures, posters and graffiti can visually encourage or dishearten the onlooker – they may even alienate or distress in extreme examples. Books, magazines, music, videos and other materials can convey supportive and encouraging messages for lesbian and gay visitors as well as for regular service users and staff.

Administration

Statistical record keeping can also become a powerful tool for chal-lenging heterosexism and helping to raise the visibility of lesbians and gay men in social work. The adoption of common procedures in the design and completion of forms and records to avoid categories such as 'marital status' or terms such as 'single', 'divorced', etc. would minimise the tendency to exclude lesbians and gay men. More accurate information will be recorded, and all staff who are made aware of the reasoning behind such practices will be exposed to more inclusive thinking towards lesbians and gay men.

The following checklist may be useful in ensuring that lesbian and gay issues are central to policy and practice:

- What is the equal opportunity policy of your department?
- How inclusive is it of lesbian and gay sexuality?
- How were you made aware of the equal opportunity policy?
- What status does it hold within the organisation?
- How is policy carried out and maintained?
- Which staff are involved in this process?
- How can complaints be pursued?
- What training on anti-oppressive practice is available and how inclusive is this of anti-heterosexism?
- What status does the training have, i.e. voluntary/compulsory?
- What is the department policy on sexual health education?
- Does departmental policy attempt to address the tension within the law and social work practice?
- What departmental supervision and support policies are in place?
- What training is available on supervision?
- What is the policy on selection and recruitment of staff?
- How effectively does this policy take account of an anti-oppressive value base?
- What training is available about selection and recruitment processes?
- How involved are user groups in the selection of staff?
- What are the users' views on their involvement in selecting staff?

Part 2

Teaching/training material

The teaching/training session

Introduction

This part of the book offers a variety of teaching and training materials for work with individuals or with groups of students. The exercises – some developed by ourselves, others adapted from other sources – have all been used successfully with students and clearly have met their aims and objectives.

The material is presented in an accessible format that outlines the purpose of each exercise, provides instructions regarding the process and lists the necessary resources to achieve the task. 'Trainers' notes' are also included, offering suggestions about some of the issues that particular exercises should raise.

The two sample timetables (see pages 37 and 38) can be used as a guide for developing a session. Clearly every situation will differ in terms of group size and learning needs, and exercise material should be selected and/or adapted accordingly. For example, groups of people who have previously spent time together discussing personal and/or emotive issues do not need, as a rule, to formulate a new working agreement. Instead it would be more appropriate to remind them of the initial agreement they have made with each other.

The exercises have been specifically chosen to encourage students to work through a process of creating a safe learning environment before exploring their own sexuality. In this way, they can build up knowledge and gain an understanding of the way lesbian and gay sexuality has been constructed, how attitudes and legislation have contributed to the oppression of lesbians and gay men and how to analyse the impact of these factors on the assessment and provision of services for lesbians and gay men. The exercises also address the multiple oppression that some lesbians and gay service users and professional workers experience.

On page 61 there is a personal action plan which offers students the opportunity not only to reflect on and consolidate their learning experience and define any future action they might take, but also to identify future learning needs. Also included is a sample course/session evaluation questionnaire to be completed by students. Clearly monitored teaching and training provides essential information for designing and planning future sessions.

Ice breakers

After a formal introduction to the session which should include the practical arrangements for the day and the aims and objectives of the session, an 'ice breaker' exercise should be introduced to actively engage the students in the training session.

Ice breakers are useful particularly for courses which focus on personal issues and feelings, for they help group members to get to know one another and begin to develop trust, feel relaxed and more comfortable. Also, ice breakers are fun!

Although there are many different kinds of ice breakers, three are included here. The time they take to complete varies depending on the size of the group. However, as a guide, ice breakers generate the most energy when the process moves quickly and introductions are brief.

Ice breaker 1

- Arrange the group in a circle.
- Each person selects a piece of jewellery or clothing or some item from a pocket or bag – the 'something' must convey a message about the person.
- In turn each group member introduces him/herself and their object and what it says about them – e.g. a diary could mean: must remember; need to organise myself; always busy.

Ice breaker 2

- Divide the group into pairs.
- Each person introduces themselves to their partner, explaining four things about themselves.
- Each pair then joins up with three other pairs. Each person then introduces their partner to the rest of the group.

Ice breaker 3

- Arrange the group in a circle.
- Each person is given two pieces of paper, then asked to write down their worst fears about being on the course.
- The pieces of paper are collected in a box; each person picks two papers from the box and reads them out. (No comments at this stage.)
- Each participant then joins with three others; and they discuss/ share feelings about their fears (if they wish).
- Participants then go back to the large group.
- Note any comments anyone wishes to make.

Working agreements

Aim/purpose

- To ensure active participation from all group members.
- To determine a level of success from the session.
- To allow students to consider their personal learning needs.
- To enable the group to take responsibility for negotiating and setting the ground rules.
- To enable students to co-operate and work alongside each other.
- To ensure an element of safety and confidentiality.

Time

30 minutes.

Resources

- Flip chart and pen.
- Three questions written on flip chart:

  1 What do I want from this session?
  2 How will I get it?
  3 What might get in the way of achieving it?

Task

- Arrange people in pairs. Each person to spend 5 minutes answering the questions. Then share their thoughts/answers with their partner.

- Back into the large group to identify the ground rules which will enable each person to achieve their goal. Ground rules should be listed on a flip chart and remain on display throughout the session.

Additional information

Common examples of ground rules include:

- Confidentiality of information shared.
- The right to be heard.
- The right to remain silent.
- Respect.
- Constructive challenge.

Endings

Aim/purpose

- Saying goodbye.
- To mark the closing of a session.
- To reflect on the process of the session.
- To reflect on the personal learning from the session; encourage students to take responsibility for their own learning.

Time

5–10 minutes.

Resources

- Flip chart with the following three items written on it:

  1 Name.
  2 One thing I've enjoyed about today.
  3 One thing I'm taking away from the session.

Task

- Group to form as a circle. Each person in turn to address the three questions listed above.
- Note: No challenges or verbal responses to be made by other students.

Additional information

- Teachers/trainers should be sensitive to unexpected negative responses.
- An alternative ending can be the handing out of a Personal Action Plan (see below). Students to complete this by themselves before the end of the session.

Personal action plan

This has been designed to enable students to develop realistic, practical and achievable goals. It is also useful as a means of enabling them to monitor their progress.

When students are completing the action plan, it is important for them to consider knowledge, theory, values and attitudes.

1   *What are the priorities for me in terms of my personal development?*

2   *What plans and objectives can I set for myself?*

3   *How will I achieve my objectives?*

4   *What obstacles could get in the way of achieving my objectives?*

5   *How might I overcome the obstacles?*

6   *Target dates for achieving my objectives.*

7   *What resources are needed to help achieve my goal (e.g. course, practice experience, tutor, books, operational guidelines, or other relevant documents)?*

8   *Methods I will use to review and evaluate my progress.*

Evaluation questionnaire

Title of session ....

Facilitators(s) ....

Date ....

1   *How would you rate the session overall?*

	Low 0	1	2	3	4	High 5
Content						
Presentation						
Improving knowledge						
Improving skills						
Enjoyment						
Outline of the session						
Reading list						
Support materials						

2   *Did the session meet the aims and objectives?*

3   *Which section/exercise did you find particularly useful and why?*

4   *Which sections/exercises did you find unhelpful and why?*

5   *(If appropriate) Comment on the content and presentation of teaching delivered by external trainers.*

6   *Comment on the way this session addressed anti-oppressive, anti-discriminatory practice.*

7   *What improvement or changes could be made to the sessions?*

8   *Any other comments?*

Exercise **The meaning of sexuality**

Aim/purpose

- To begin to consider sexuality in view of participants' own life experience.

Time

45 minutes.

Resources

- Piece of drawing paper, coloured pens.
- Handout on sexuality (Bremner and Hillin, 1993, p. 14).

Task

- Participants to move into groups of four. They should work by themselves and write or draw something that reflects what the word sexuality means to them (5 minutes).
- Discuss drawing/image with other group members (20 minutes).
- The small group to then produce a drawing that represents their collective idea of what sexuality means (20 minutes)
- A group drawing to be displayed on the wall (the market place) for other groups to consider at their leisure.

Additional information

- Individual ideas might be organised in terms of feelings, attitudes, behaviour, relationships, abuse etc.
- Small groups may wish to consider which aspects of their sexuality they allow or deny.
- Remind students to consider aspect of gender, race, disability, culture, religion, age.

Exercise   **Thinking about your own sexuality**

Aim/purpose

- To give participants the opportunity to reflect on the development of their own sexuality and the impact this has had on their lives.

Time

45–60 minutes.

Resources

- 'Sexuality questionnaire' on page 65.
- 'Trainers' notes' (see pages 65–7).

Task

- Distribute questionnaire and ask participants to consider the questions individually (10 minutes).
- Optional: Depending on whether the group members have had the chance to get to know each other, ask participants to talk with a partner about their responses to the questions.
- Note: They are not being asked to share all their answers (15 minutes).
- The trainer goes through the range of possible responses with the group, highlighting the information supplied in the 'Trainers' notes' (20 minutes)
- Participants are invited to comment or ask questions about the exercise.

Additional information

- Stress that participants may omit any questions which are likely to cause them any distress.
- Decide in advance on your terms when discussing the possible range of situations experienced by lesbians and gay men. As an 'out' lesbian or gay trainer, you may wish to say 'we'; for heterosexual trainers and lesbian and gay workers who are not 'out' in this setting, be careful not to continually say 'they' with all that this may convey.

Sexuality questionnaire

1 How would you describe your sexual orientation: e.g. lesbian/ gay; heterosexual; celibate; bisexual?
2 When did you first recognise or become aware of your sexuality?
3 Has your sense of your own sexuality or your sexual orientation changed since your first awareness?
4 What has influenced the development of your sexuality?
5 Is your sexuality acceptable to you, your family, friends and colleagues?
6 How openly can you express your sexuality; a) at home; b) at work; c) in public?
7 What effect might your sexuality have on your professional practice?

Trainers' notes

This is just a starting point. Other information can be added by drawing on material elsewhere in this book as well as newspaper articles and other reading. It is also useful to talk with lesbians and gay men themselves about their experiences.

The following points relate to the items in the Sexuality Questionnaire:

1 Heterosexuals are rarely required to declare their orientation; it is taken to be the norm and assumed unless information is given to the contrary. Celibacy is not strictly an orientation; although often used as a term in this context, lesbians, gay men and heterosexuals may declare themselves to be celibate. Sexual orientation may also include less socially desirable terms, such as paedophile, so care may need to be exercised when statements endorsing choice are emphasised.

The use of terms such as lesbians or gay usually implies a sense of identity; it is important to remember that many more people may have homosexual encounters or engage in homosexual behaviour without ever calling themselves lesbian or gay.
2 Thoughts about sexuality are not necessarily the same as a first sexual experience. Children may often experience sexual feeling at a young age, although for some, their first awareness may have been as a result of abuse.
3 For heterosexuals, there is sometimes a taken for granted quality

about their development; while some lesbians and gay men may say they have always known, others may come to an awareness of their sexual feeling much later on in life, many after years of marriage or long-term heterosexual relationships and having had children. Other changes may occur through life as a result of changing views of relationships, one's own body or different views about sexual behaviour.

4   The debate about the origins of lesbian or gay behaviour continues in various guises, broadly within a nature–nurture dichotomy. The nurture arguments often focus on negative experiences in early childhood – watch out for mother blaming! There is also the question of choice emphasised by radical feminists, who might make a political decision not to have sexual relationships with men. The overwhelming 'pressure' in terms of socialisation is of course to the heterosexual media, role expectations, etc. Contrary to what is sometimes thought, there is no evidence that the children of lesbians or gay men are more likely to grow up as lesbian or gay – after all, most lesbians and gay men grew up in heterosexual families!

5   It is highly unlikely that heterosexuality will be a surprise to others, within the family, socially or at work – indeed, social expectations are built around the idea of getting an opposite-sex partner, going out to social events as a couple, dealing with insurance and housing, etc., on this basis. Humour is frequently homophobic in its stereotypical and derogatory images of homosexual behaviour.

Lesbians and gay men may encounter a very different response when declaring their sexuality, whether this is coming out to family, friends or colleagues. Sometimes it may be OK to be 'out' in one setting, but not another.

The level of homophobia in society may make it particularly difficult for young people to accept their sense of themselves as lesbian or gay, leading to feelings of shame or guilt internalised oppression.

6   The public expression of affection between same-sex couples is disapproved of and on occasions may lead to police action. Compare this to the frequent sight of heterosexual couples kissing, cuddling or simply walking down the street holding hands. Pinning up posters, pictures or wearing badges connected with being lesbian or gay may also present difficulties in social or work settings.

7   Despite the many publicised cases of abuse committed by men against women, there remains the stereotyped view of gay men in particular representing a threat to children. The clear distinction

between gay men and paedophiles is often overlooked when gay men apply for work with children or young people, leaving them in the difficult position of having to decide whether to be out or not. Lesbians also face similar views as to their being a threat to young women.

The attitudes of managers, practice teachers and anyone in a position of authority at work may make a difference between feeling relaxed and safe at work, and hence able to get on with the work, or being frightened of discovery or accused of unprofessional behaviour. There is also the question of the extent to which support may be available within the organisation, especially if subjected to harassment or prejudice by colleagues or service users. Heterosexuals in general are unlikely to have to consider these issues, at least not in any potentially problematic way.

Exercise **Your own sexuality**

Aim/purpose

- To give participants the opportunity to identify and explore the sexual messages they received as young children.
- To understand how these messages have influenced their own sexuality (i.e., attitudes, values and behaviour).
- To explore their perceptions and understanding of the idea of normal sexual development.

Time

45 minutes.

Resources

- Pens and paper.

Task

- Participants to sit with a partner with whom they feel able to share personal information.
- First, participants to spend time alone to consider the messages they received as a child about sexuality and where those messages came from (10 minutes).

- Then participants make a note/draw a picture or design symbols to represent the messages.
- Second, participants in pairs spend 20 minutes (10 minutes each, uninterrupted) to share as much as they feel able before moving on to a discussion about how these messages have influenced their own sexuality.
- Then participants compare similar and different experiences (10 minutes).
- Participants rejoin as a whole group and are invited to comment or share own personal experience if they wish (5 minutes).

Additional information

- As a variation to the exercise, participants can identify the messages about the development of sexuality by drawing a time line or life map.

Exercise   Images of lesbian and gay relationships

Aim/purpose

- To identify and discuss different aspects of lesbian and gay relationships.
- To identify personal attitudes, values, and stereotypical assumptions of lesbians and gay men.

Time

30 minutes.

Resources

- Selection of photographs (taken from newspapers, cards, photographs or copied from books) which depict positive images of lesbians and gay men.

Task

- Participants divided into small groups; each group to be given a set of photographs, which are then spread out on the floor.

- Group members to look at all the photographs until they find one that either gives a strong message or raises issues (positive or negative) for them.
- In turn, each person has 2 minutes to discuss the chosen photograph and its meaning/or issue raised for them. Other students then respond.
- Participants then return to the large group for any feedback on the process or discussion of the issues raised.

Additional information

- What feelings do the photographs provoke?
- What have students learned about homosexuality?
- How will what they have learned affect their practice?

Exercise Myths about lesbians and gay men

Aim/purpose

- To enable participants to confront their prejudice and false beliefs.

Time

30 minutes.

Resources

- 'Trainers' notes' (see page 70).
- Flip chart paper, marker pens, Blu-Tack.

Task

- Participants divided into small groups (four to six people).
- Each group member to consider: how they felt/reacted when they first heard about lesbians and gay men.
- Each small group to list statements/words they have heard people say about lesbians and gay men; then to list these statements on flip chart under the headings *Lesbians, Gay men, Bisexuals*.
- Lesbians and gay men should be considered separately.

- Small groups to return to beginning group, and each group to give feedback.
- Flip chart papers to be Blu-Tacked on to walls of meeting room.
- Participants to work through the statements and where necessary to challenge the truth of each statement.

Trainers' notes

This is a list of statements students have raised about lesbians and gay men. You will need to be able to identify these and the myths they are associated with. For example, myth: gay men are child molesters; answer: the majority of child molesters are (97 per cent) heterosexual men.

Lesbians	Gay men	Bisexuals
Feminist	Child molester	Best of both worlds
Men haters	Promiscuous	Frigid
Butch/femme	Uncommitted	Oversexed
Masculine	Queer	Indecisive
Invisible	Benders	AIDS risk
Asexual	Perverted	Deviant
Aggressive	Creative	Weird
Oversexed/predatory	Effeminate	Betrayal
Small minority	Unnatural	Trendy
Can't have children	Women haters	White
White	White	Middle class
Middle class	Middle class	Able bodied
Able bodied	Able bodied	
Act like men	Shirt lifters	
Not oppressed	All of them have AIDS	
Hormone problem	Dress like women	
Unnatural	Make good friends	
Sick	Sensitive	
Dress like men	Artistic	
All alike	Sinners	

Exercise **Sexuality awareness**

Aim/purpose

- To enable participants to establish a level of knowledge about lesbians and gay men; and to begin to demystify lesbian and gay lifestyles.
- To identify any confusion about relevant legislation that impacts on lesbian and gay lifestyles.
- To highlight the conflicts and inconsistencies between legislation and anti-oppressive social work practice when working with lesbians and gay men.

Resources

- Handout 'Sexuality awareness quiz', on pages 72–3.
- 'Trainers' answers.

Task

- Students to work through the questions alone.
- In small groups or with their practice teacher, students to discuss those questions they found most difficult to answer.
- Back in the large group, participants address any differences of opinion/values held. Discuss the implications of the issues raised for social work practice and for working with lesbian and gay service users in an anti-oppressive way.

Additional information

- At the time of writing this book, the answers given on the questionnaire were correct. However, teachers need to be aware of possible changes in legislation and correct the responses accordingly.
- This exercise is very flexible and can take as much time as necessary. It offers an opportunity for students to explore issues in depth or to increase their awareness in preparation for a more in-depth discussion at a later stage.

Sexuality awareness quiz

1   When was homosexuality legalised in England and Wales?

   1967   1971   1955   1933   **[Ans: 1967 Sexual Offences Act]**

2   What is the age of consent for gay men in England?

   18   25   21   16   **[Ans: 18]**

3   What is the age of consent for lesbians in Britain?

   18   16   21   Other   **[Ans: 16]**

4   What percentage of the population is generally thought to be lesbian or gay?

   20%   10%   1.5%   7%   **[Ans: 10%]**

5   If you are openly gay or lesbian, from which of the following jobs are you barred by law?

   Soldier   Police officer   Prison officer   RAF pilot   Judge
   [Ans: All]

6   Most transvestites (men who dress up in female clothing) are gay?

   True   False   **[Ans: False]**

7   Local authorities are banned from intentionally promoting homosexuality under which act of Parliament?

   Indecency Act   Sexual Offences Act   Local Government Act
   Children Act   **[Ans: Local Government Act]**

8   Which of the following 'soaps' has not had an openly gay/lesbian character?

   EastEnders   Coronation Street   Emmerdale Farm   Brookside
   [Ans: Coronation Street]

9   Within many walks of life there are increasingly people who have come out as gay or lesbian. Can you name a famous person who is openly gay or lesbian from the following areas?

   Sports person   Member of Parliament   Actor/actress
   Pop singer

10   Who refused to acknowledge that lesbians existed?

The Queen Mother   Margaret Thatcher   Queen Victoria
Winston Churchill   **[Ans: Queen Victoria]**

11   Is it legal for gay men and lesbians to foster children?

Yes   No   **[Ans: Yes]**

12   Is it legal for gay men and lesbians to adopt children?

Yes   No   **[Ans: Yes]**

13   In which of the following countries is it legal for same-sex
couples to marry?

Sweden Holland Poland Ireland Hungary   **[Ans: Sweden]**

14   What colour triangles were gay and lesbian internees made to
wear in the Nazi concentration camps?

Purple   Black   Pink   Green   White   **[Ans: Black, Pink]**

15   True or False? It is illegal to dismiss someone from their job solely
because they are gay or lesbian?

True   False   **[Ans: True]**

16   In 1968 the Stonewall riots marked a change in the official
attitude to gay and lesbian rights, in which country?

Australia   Canada   South Africa   US   Scotland   **[Ans: US]**

17   In whose reign was homosexuality first made a crime?

Elizabeth I   Henry III   Queen Victoria   James I
                                                [Ans: Queen Victoria]

18   Can same-sex couples be punished by law for openly showing
affection in public places?

Yes   No   **[Ans: Yes]**

Exercise **Heterosexuality**

Aim/purpose

- To enable participants to consider their own sexuality and what is 'normal' about heterosexuality.
- To realise that the questions listed on pages 75–6 are the same as those presented to lesbians and gay men by people who assume that their heterosexuality is 'normal'.

Time

- Will depend on how the questionnaire is used. See additional information below.

Resources

- Handout 'Heterosexuality questionnaire' (pages 75–6).

Task

- Initially each student to work through the questionnaire alone; then in small groups to discuss those questions they found confusing or too difficult to answer.

Additional information

- This exercise is very flexible in terms of the amount of time needed to enable students to complete the questionnaire. It can be used as a long or short exercise depending on the level of discussion about the issues raised. It is equally effective with individuals working alone or with groups.
- The exercise is useful in dispelling some of the myths that influence the way lesbian and gay men are perceived and judged.
- It offers an opportunity to raise awareness of some issues that affect lesbians and gay men, thus preparing the ground for a more in-depth discussion at a later stage.

Heterosexuality questionnaire

Gay people get asked some pretty strange questions. Often this is because their interrogators have a narrow, strictly heterosexual view of what is normal. The November 1989 issue of *New Internationalist* turned the tables by asking heterosexual people some strange questions too ...

1   What do you think is the cause of your heterosexuality?

2   When did you first realise you might be heterosexual?

3   Have you told your parents and what do they think of it?

4   Are there others like you in your family?

5   Would you say that you had an inadequate mother or father figure?

6   Don't you think your heterosexuality might be a phase you are going through?

7   Are you afraid of members of your own sex?

8   Isn't it possible that what you need is a good gay lover?

9   What do you actually do in bed?

10   You put what where?

11   But how can people of the opposite sex really please each other when there are such vast emotional and biological differences between them?

12   Although society gives considerable support to the institution of marriage, the divorce rate is spiralling. Why are there so few stable relationships among heterosexuals?

13   Is it because heterosexuals are so promiscuous?

14   There seem to be very few happy heterosexuals. Have you considered aversion therapy?

15   Why do you feel compelled to seduce others into your sexual activities?

16   Why do you insist on making such a public spectacle of your heterosexuality? Can't you just keep quiet about it?

17   More than 90 per cent of child molesters are thought to be heterosexuals. Would you feel comfortable about entrusting your children's education to heterosexual teachers?

18   Why do people like you emphasize the heterosexual qualities of famous people such as film stars? Is it because you need to validate your own condition?

19   Penetrative sex is most common among heterosexual couples. Aren't you worried about the risk of getting AIDS?

20   If everybody were heterosexual like you, what would happen to the world's population? Don't you think it is rather unreasonable and irresponsible of you to insist on sleeping with people of the opposite sex?

© *New Internationalist*, November, 1989

Exercise   **Your move**

Aim/purpose

- To enable participants to consider their own sexuality.
- To consider what is 'normal' about heterosexuality. To realise that these same questions lesbians and gay men are constantly being asked by people who assume their own heterosexuality is 'normal'.

Time

30 minutes

Resources

- Room large enough for participants to move about.

- 'Your move' question sheet on pages 77–8.
- A card for each student indicating who they are – for example: a prostitute; a black heterosexual woman/man; a gay man; a drug user; a single parent; a 15-year-old gay teenager; a young lesbian; an older man; someone living with AIDS; a person with special needs; a white heterosexual woman/man.

Task

- Each person is given a card indicating who they are; but they are to keep their identity to themselves for the first part of this exercise.
- Everyone in the group should stand in a straight line, with their backs to the wall.
- The facilitator calls out the questions from the question sheet.
- Individuals respond if their answer to the question is 'yes' by taking one step forward. Alternatively if their response is 'no', they remain standing where they are.
- When all the questions have been asked, individuals remain in their positions and look around to check where each person is standing.
- Each person is then asked to reveal who they are.

Additional information

Issues to be raised in the discussion should include:

- How it feels to be in the position you are in?
- What impact does this position have on the person and those close to him/her?
- What is the justification for the position people find themselves in?

'Your move' question sheet

1 Can you speak positively about your sexuality in school?

2 Is your sexuality viewed as illegal?

3 Are you comfortable in being honest about your sexuality with colleagues in work?

4   Do you feel safe walking in the streets after dark?

5   Can you take your partner to social events at work?

6   Can you legally have sex with more than one person at a time?

7   Can you hold your partner's hand in the street without fear of physical or verbal abuse?

8   Could you legally sign the consent form if your partner needed emergency medical treatment?

9   Is your sexuality considered suitable for a person with responsibility for children?

10   Can you expect to be treated fairly by the police?

11   Can you become a judge?

12   Are you sure your children will not face discrimination at school?

13   If your partner died, would you automatically be recognised as the next of kin?

14   Could you get private health insurance without too much difficulty?

15   If you wished, could you join the Merchant Navy?

16   Are people like you welcomed in church?

17   If you so desired, could you legally have sex with your partner in a hotel bedroom?

18   Could you and your partner legally marry in a church or registry office?

19   Would it be easy for you to introduce your partner to your family?

Exercise Denial of rights

Aim/purpose

- To explore issues arising from work with lesbian and gay service users.
- Lesbian and gay workers to develop strategies for anti-discriminatory/anti-oppressive social work practice.
- Workers to identify areas of the law that oppress and discriminate against lesbians and gay men.

Resources

- Flip chart and pens.
- 'Trainers' notes' (page 80).
- List of areas in which lesbians and gay men experience discrimination and oppression (i.e. the law, the family, on the street, social work, children, housing, health, finance).

Task

- Divide into small groups and discuss the discrimination lesbians and gay men experience in each area.
- Return to the large group and fill in the list on a flip chart.

Additional information

- Point out the relevance of this exercise for social work practice – for example, how workers will encounter these difficulties when advocating on behalf of lesbian and gay service users, working with other professionals and organisations.

Trainers' notes

Listed below are some examples of discrimination experienced by lesbians and gay men in various areas.

The law

- Age of consent
- Residence order
- Parent/child contact
- Donor insemination

Finance

- No tax allowance
- Cohabitation
- Inheritance
- Insurance

Housing

- Non-inheritance of tenancies
- Obtaining tenancies
- Harassment

Health

- AIDS
- Contraception/pregnancy
- Mental health
- Stress/isolation
- Death

Children

- Residence/contact
- Discrimination at school
- Social worker's attitude
- Adoption and fostering

The family

- Inheritance
- Disputes/rifts
- Disowned by

On the street

- Attacks
- Victimisation
- Murder

Social

- Lack of facilities
- Lack of recognition
- Lack of financial support

Work

- Harassment
- Employment
- Compassionate leave
- Double life
- Isolation/stress
- Criminal record
- Unfair dismissal
- Armed forces

Exercise Card game

Aim/purpose

- To consider the ways in which the law discriminates against lesbians and gay men.
- To recognise how the civil rights of lesbians and gay men are denied.
- To highlight the oppression lesbians and gay men experience throughout their life.
- To highlight some everyday situations heterosexuals take for granted.

Time

- 30 minutes to play cards.
- 15 minutes for large-group feedback/discussion.

Resources

- Copy and cut out a set of cards (see pages 82–4).
- 'Trainers' notes' (see pages 85–7).

Task

- Divide into small groups of four to five people.
- Hand out a set of cards to each group.
- The person with card 1 starts and reads out the question.
- The group agrees the answer and follows the instruction on each card.

Additional information

- Each question should be considered in respect of Jo, Bobby, Leslie, George and Chris being: 1) heterosexual, 2) lesbian or 3) gay.
- The final decision in responding to the question on the card should reflect circumstances for lesbians or gay men.
- If the students answer the questions correctly, the cards should form a full circle and no cards will remain.

Sample cards

Card 1

Sam and Jo jointly own a property and are tenants in common. If Sam dies, does Jo automatically inherit Sam's share of the property?

Yes	Go to card 10
No	Go to card 6

Card 2

Can Sam and Jo kiss in public without fear of arrest?

Yes	Go to card 1
No	Go to card 11

Card 3

Leslie sleeps in an attic bedroom. Jo and Bobby sleep in a first floor bedroom and want to have sex. Is Leslie in danger of police prosecution?

Yes	Go to card 14
No	Go to card 8

Card 4

Chris is 16 and George is 19. They have been in a relationship for three months and decide they want to have sex. Is this illegal?

Yes	Go to card 15
No	Go to card 10

Card 5

Chris and George want to discuss the following issues: their sexuality, living together and information about safer sex. They decide to raise these issues with their sixth form tutor. Would all schools support this?

Yes	Go to card 3
No	Go to card 9

Card 6

Jo and Bobby are both in full-time, permanent employment and want to apply for a mortgage with insurance cover. Could you foresee any immediate difficulties with their request?

Yes	Go to card 13
No	Go to card 7

Card 7

Jo lives with Bobby in his flat. If Bobby dies, does Jo have automatic right to succession to the tenancy?

| Yes | Go to card 2 |
| No | Go to card 3 |

Card 8

Pat was born in Britain and Di in Sweden. They married and have lived in Stockholm for the past 10 years. Due to promotion at work, Pat has to move to England. Di intends to follow. Will the law allow them to live together permanently?

| Yes | Go to card 7 |
| No | Go to card 5 |

Card 9

Does Section 28 of the Local Government Act 1988, restrict lifestyle, visibility and choice for Pat and Di?

| Yes | Go to card 4 |
| No | Go to card 1 |

Card 10

Bobby and Jo have been in a stable relationship for 8 years and want to have a child through donor insemination. They intend to contact a clinic. Will donor insemination be legally possible?

| Yes | Go to card 11 |
| No | Go to card 4 |

Card 11

Jo has a baby and Bobby requests appropriate leave from work. The organisation has an equal opportunities policy. Do you envisage any problems with Bobby's request?

| Yes | Go to card 8 |
| No | Go to card 15 |

Card 12

Jo is rushed into hospital and needs emergency treatment, but is too ill to consent to this. Bobby agrees to sign the form. Will Bobby's signature be acceptable?

| Yes | Go to card 6 |
| No | Go to card 14 |

Card 13

Jo and Bobby continue in their long term, loving relationship. Unable to have their own child, they decide to apply to the local authority to adopt a child. Do you envisage any problems if they apply?

Yes	Go to card 12
No	Go to card 2

Card 14

Di has a ten-year-old child called Sam. Pat has co-parented Sam for nine years. Di is concerned to secure Sam's future with Pat in the event of her death ... Might this raise some difficulties?

Yes	Go to card 5
No	Go to card 12

Card 15

Jo and Bobby are nearing retirement. Bobby has a pension from work and has paid National Insurance contributions for the past 40 years. If Bobby died suddenly, would these pension rights be automatically transferred to Jo?

Yes	Go to card 9
No	Go to card 13

Trainers' notes

Card 1: Answer *no*

If there is no Will to say otherwise, Sam's share of the property passes by the rules of inheritance to his/her next of kin (and that's not Jo).

Card 2: Answer *no*

Gay men holding hands or kissing in public can be charged under the 1956 Sexual Offences Act, Section 32 regarding gross indecency. Lesbians and gay men can be charged under Section 5 of the 1986 Public Order Act which prohibits disorderly, abusive or threatening behaviour likely to cause public alarm or distress.

Card 3: Answer *yes*

Gay men can be charged under the 1967 Sexual Offences Act if they have sex in a place where other people have access or could come across them. Leslie may therefore also be prosecuted. Only if one lesbian is under 16 years and the other 16 years or over can the older person be charged with an assault.

Card 4: Answer *yes*

The age of consent for heterosexual men, women and lesbians is 16 years; for gay men, 18 years.

Card 5: Answer *no*

The 1986 Education Act talks about moral consideration and family life. Circular 11/87 Department of Education and Science, 1987, says that 'sex education lessons must be set with a clear moral framework … no place in any school in any circumstances for teaching which advocates homosexual behaviour or which presents it as the norm; or which encourages homosexual experimentation by pupils'.

Card 6: Answer *yes*

Insurance companies, panicking about HIV/AIDS, generally insist that if two males want to buy a property jointly, they may be turned down or required to take an HIV test before insurance cover is granted. If either of the men has already had a test and the insurance company finds out, then they most probably will be turned down.

Card 7: Answer *no*

The 1980 Housing Act gives the surviving partner of a relationship the right to succeed to the tenancy, but this does not apply to lesbian and gay couples.

Card 8: Answer *no*

The foreign partners of British lesbians and gay men have no right to establish permanent residence in this country.

Card 9: Answer *yes*

It affects lesbians and gay men but not heterosexuals.

Card 10: Answer *no*

The Human Fertilisation and Embryology Act 1990 says that clinics have to be licensed to provide donor insemination and need to take into account before providing a service the welfare of any child who might be born as a result of the treatment ... including the need of that child for a father.

Note: This Act does not affect private arrangements.

Card 11: Answer *yes*

Although many organisations have equal opportunities policies, rarely do they afford the same rights to lesbian and gay partners as they do for heterosexual partners.

Card 12: Answer *no*

Because the law does not recognise lesbian and gay relationships, lesbian and gay partners have no legal rights with regard to Next of Kin or visiting rights in hospital (or prison).

Card 13: Answer *yes*

Although the emphasis is now on the best interests of the child and on the government's focus on family values, lesbians and gay men will face restrictions when being considered as adopters because of their chosen way of life.

Card 14: Answer *yes*

There are no immediate legal restrictions. However, judges often insist on normal family life as essential to the well-being of the child. Consequently, lesbians and gay men are more often than not seen as unsuitable parents.

Card 15: Answer *no*

The law does not recognise long-term lesbian and gay relationships – therefore lesbian and gay partners have no rights with regard to taxation and inheritance.

Exercise   **Rights of passage**

Aim/purpose

- To help students, practice teachers and tutors look at how lesbian and gay experiences of rights of passage are invalidated.

Time

30 minutes.

Resources

- Video, *Torch Song Trilogy* (Fierstein, 1989).

Task

- Divide into small groups (four people). Each person to identify and list important 'ceremonies' they have taken part in and what the ceremonies meant for them.
- Each group then discusses ceremonies and the issues raised.
- Back in the large group, all participants watch the sequence from *Torch Song Trilogy* where mother and son are in the grave-yard.
- General discussion of issues raised.

Additional information

- Issues to be addressed would include: the validity of ceremonies, approval by society and the acceptance of a process of grieving following the loss of a loved one.
- These issues to be considered from a lesbian and gay perspective.

Exercise **Sexuality and social work practice**

Aim/purpose

- To consider how issues relating to sexuality may present themselves in practice and to discuss any dilemmas which may arise.

Time

40–60 minutes.

Resources

- Copies of 'Case studies' (pages 89–92).
- 'Trainers' notes' (pages 92–5).

Task

- Divide participants into small groups of four to six people. Distribute case studies; depending on time, one or two studies per group.
- Ask small groups to work on one or two scenarios, identifying issues and considering how social workers/probation officers might respond, including examples of poor practice as well as good (20 minutes for each scenario).
- Depending on the size of the group overall, organise feedback and raise the questions listed under General issues.

General issues

- How to deal with dilemmas and conflicts with personal moral/religious beliefs.
- Consider the support you might get from supervisors: what to do if their views are in conflict with yours or are homophobic?

- Your understanding of guidelines for good practice.
- Contact/information re gay and lesbian organisations.

Note: This exercise should be preceded by a general introduction to the issue, appropriate input, etc.

Case studies

For each case study, consider what issues need to be addressed.

Case study 1: John

John is in his fifties and recently had a brief admission to hospital for treatment for depression. He lives alone and is generally in poor health. The information you have from the hospital social worker is that until recently John lived with a long-standing partner, Frank. He is now very isolated, his only source of support are his neighbours, Jackie and Dave, where he regularly babysits for their four children.

The GP has referred John to social services, requesting domiciliary and social support.

Case study 2: Paula

Paula is divorced with a four-year-old son. She is on probation and you have met with her on several occasions. So far she has not been very forthcoming during your meetings but you have had no particular cause for concern.

The health visitor involved with Paula and her child has now contacted you, saying that she has reason to believe that Paula is a lesbian.

Case study 3: Gurnam

Gurnam is 16 and currently in an assessment centre following several incidents of taking vehicles without consent. Last weekend he absconded from the unit for several days and was returned by the police who are making no further charges. They have, however, alleged that Gurnam was seen hanging around a well-known gay bar and comment that he appears to be in possession of rather large sums of money.

What are the main issues to be addressed?

Case study 4: Ben

Ben is 15 and has lived with foster carers for three years. They have strong Evangelical Christian beliefs. Ben has been arrested following a consenting sexual encounter with an older man in a public lavatory and charged with gross indecency.

The foster carers are anxious and unsure about continuation of the placement. Ben is concerned about going to court and the implications for his long-term placement. What are the main issues to be addressed, and how might your feelings affect your assessment and intervention?

Case study 5: Sarah

You are requested to do an assessment on Sarah, a women in her late seventies, who is experiencing increasing difficulty in maintaining herself at home. The referral indicates that she is living with her sister. When you visit the home, you find that it is a one bedroomed flat and that the two women are not related and are, in fact, in a relationship. One of them is clearly in need of intensive care of a residential nature.

What issues would need to be addressed?

Case study 6: Andrew

Senga, a colleague who works at your centre, asks your advice. She has been working closely with Andrew who is 17 and asking her support over a very distressing problem.

Some time ago Andrew met a 50-year-old man called John, and they began a sexual liaison by mutual consent. However, Andrew no longer wishes to continue this relationship but feels unable to extricate himself from it. He says that John pleads with him not to end the relationship and offers him both gifts and money quite regularly. Andrew now finds John's sexual demands 'disgusting' and wants to be left alone. Senga also explains that Andrew's developmental age is around 12 years.

Andrew is adamant that he does not want his parents involved and will not hear of the matter being referred to the police. He is asking Senga to accompany him to confront John directly; however, it is clear that she will probably be the one to do the 'confronting'.

What are the issues this raises?

Case study 7: Shahla

You are a student on placement in a mixed unit for young people. The resident group consists of five males aged 12 to 16 years and one young woman called Shahla, aged 13 years.

Over the past two weeks you have noticed a distinct change in her dress and appearance. On a number of occasions she has told the staff that she does not want to be a girl and would prefer to be a boy instead. You know her comments have been ignored by the staff.

Case study 8: Peter

Peter is 18 and has learning difficulties. He attends a local day centre. His mother contacts you by phone and asks you to visit her urgently. When you visit, she is extremely upset and demands that Peter goes into hospital for treatment because she can no longer cope with him.

Eventually she tells you the staff at the centre discovered Peter engaging in sexual activity with Alan, a 20-year-old man who recently started at the centre. She said the staff at the centre were 'quite kind about it', but she could have 'died of shame'. She has tried to speak to Peter about the incident, but he refuses to discuss it with her and goes out when she brings the subject up.

Is there any cause for concern about the incident? What course of action would you take?

Case study 9: Nancy

Nancy is a colleague in the psychiatric team at the local hospital. You have known her for some time, like her and respect her professionalism. Nancy has recently come out as a lesbian, having told you and the other team members and begins to wear a badge which features an Amazonian double-headed axe (commonly known as a lesbian symbol).

Nancy tells you that she is beginning to have 'problems' with the consultant on her ward. He is making snide remarks about lesbians and gay men, including references to them being emotionally undeveloped. Even more recently, one of her clients has told her that she refuses to work with 'a filthy dyke'.

What issues does this raise?

Case study 10: Ali and Jez

You are a student on placement in a residential unit. One afternoon you hear a noise in one of the upstairs rooms and when you investigate the cause, you find two of the boys in bed together – one aged 15 and the other 17 years old.

What issues might need to be addressed?

Case study 11: Brid

Part 1:
Brid, 35-year-old mother of two boys (aged nine and six), shares a home with a man and a woman.

Brid has been diagnosed as having inoperable cancer and her prognosis is extremely poor. Over a period of time you have been involved in counselling her and helping her make plans for her children's future. The eldest boy has been displaying disruptive behaviour at home and at school. He has been very aggressive to the others who live in the house and has stated on several occasions that he hates living there and wants to go and live with his dad. Both boys visit their father once a month.

You are a hospital social worker and visit Brid; she is extremely upset and tells you that the natural father has heard about her illness and is applying to the court for a residence order. She says quite adamantly that there is no way she would let her children live with him.

What issues are raised at this stage?

Part 2:
The first court hearing has taken place to determine the future residency of the children. As social worker you have been asked by the court to do an assessment on the children's current living situation.

On your next visit to begin the assessment, Brid tells you that she has been in a long-term relationship with the woman in the house and that the male friend is gay. It is her wish that her children are cared for by this couple, in the event of her death.

Issues to be addressed?

Trainers' notes

The following issues should be addressed in discussion about the cases.

Case study 1: John

- Loss and grief
- Depression and sexuality
- Threat to neighbours' children
- Confidentiality – open recording
- Poor health – HIV/AIDS
- Isolation
- Raising issues of sexuality
- Family contact
- Contact with gay organisations

Case study 2: Paula

- Evidence for her being lesbian?
- Legal father and residence issues
- Age/gender of child – starting school soon
- Referral to social services – child care practice
- Risk to child's development, moral danger
- Gender of worker
- Support from family
- Other sources of support

Case study 3: Gurnam

- What is being done to him – care staff/peers
- Prior sexual abuse
- Expression of sexuality
- Risk to other young boys
- Family
- Safer sex
- HIV/AIDS
- Counselling – for what

Case study 4: Ben

- Legal issues
- Placement
- Tension between religious beliefs and strong moral views
- Selection, training, support of foster carers
- Impact of own values
- Young people and sexuality
- Safer sex
- HIV/AIDS

Case study 5: Sarah

- Assumptions about the relationship
- Placement issues
- Resources to pay for care – i.e., home
- Attitudes to older people and sex/sexuality
- Historical perspective of women

Case study 6: Andrew

- Legal issues
- Consent and power
- Advocacy
- Disability and sexuality
- Internalised oppression
- Role of worker/collusion
- Gender issues

Case study 7: Shahla

- Identity
- Stereotype images of young women
- Race
- Gender
- Advocacy

Case study 8: Peter

- Disability/sexuality
- Legal issues
- Pathologising of gay men
- Advocacy
- Who is the client?

Case study 9: Nancy

- Hierarchy within a multidisciplinary team
- Homophobia
- Pathologising of lesbians
- Grievance procedure
- Equal opportunities policy
- Staff training

Case study 10: Ali and Jez

- Legal issues
- Gender
- Question child protection issues
- Group dynamics within home
- Staff policy, practice, training
- What if two girls were found together?

Case study 11: Brid

Part 1:

- Loss/bereavement
- Legal issues
- Contact and residence
- Boy's behaviour

Part 2:

- Children's wishes/feelings regarding the Children Act 1989
- Parental responsibility
- Appropriate legal representative for Brid
- Emotions of worker
- Loss/bereavement regarding partner/friend

Exercise   Sally and Jane

Aim/purpose

- To help students, practice teachers and tutors develop their anti-oppressive practice in working with lesbians and gay men.
- Note: This exercise is particularly useful for practice teacher/student on placement.

Time

Dependent on size of group.

Resources

- Copies of the case study on pages 96–8.

- 'Trainers' notes' on pages 98–9.
- Flip chart/paper/pens for each group.

Task

The following is an example of how the material can be used with a group of 12 students:

- Divide into four groups of three people, giving each group member a different role: a) Sally, b) Jane, c) Natalie.
- Each group reads the case study and 'charts up' how they would feel in their particular role (5 minutes).
- Small groups re-assemble for feedback to the whole group (5 minutes).
- Small groups 'de-role' at this point.
- Facilitator charts up any feelings/conflicts identified by the group.
- Once the students have had a chance to consider the process and the impact on Sally, Jane and Natalie, go back to the referral point and consider the facts of the case. If they were the social worker, would they have dealt with things differently?

Additional information

- Caution: Either in a one-to-one or in a group situation, the practice teacher/facilitator needs to be aware that individual(s) working on the exercise may be a lesbian mother or a gay parent. Therefore this exercise may evoke strong feelings.

Case study of Sally and Jane

Sally and Jane have been in a stable relationship for the past nine years. They have both been married and between them have three children. The family became involved with social services three years ago.

Sally, concerned for the safety of her 13-year-old-daughter Natalie (one of two girls), made a self-referral to social services. Natalie had started staying out all night, and on one occasion had been missing for three days. At the initial meeting with the social worker Sally and Jane were very open about their relationship. Because of the difficulties they were experiencing with Natalie, they requested respite care for her for two to three weeks, in order for 'things to calm down'.

The social worker told them there were no beds available in any residential unit and suggested that as an alternative a referral could be made to the family therapy unit where they would be given the opportunity to discuss and resolve their difficulties. Desperate for help, both Sally and Jane agreed to attend. At the first meeting with the psychologist, they were invited to outline the problems. A second meeting was arranged at a time convenient for everyone.

The day before the second meeting, the psychologist telephoned Sally to explain that it would have to be cancelled. The meeting was rearranged for a time when Jane was unable to attend. Sally agreed to go on her own with Natalie. During the course of the meeting, Sally became emotionally distraught and stressed and said she had failed as a mother and blamed her relationship with Jane for Natalie's behaviour.

This was the only meeting Sally had with the psychologist, who never contacted her again. However, following the meeting, it was agreed that Natalie should be accommodated in a short-stay residential unit. On the day when Natalie was admitted to the unit, she was accompanied by Jane.

The first review was held within two weeks of Natalie's admission, and both Sally and Jane attended the meeting. It was suggested that there should be a planned return home for Natalie and that the process should begin by her having one overnight stay per week at home. Sally agreed to this arrangement but was not convinced that the time was right for Natalie to return home and felt under immense pressure from the workers at the residential unit.

Natalie's overnight stays were very problematic, and her relationship with Sally was very unsatisfactory. Sally felt that the return home had been premature even though she wanted Natalie to return home to live at some point in the future. Nonetheless, at the next meeting at the unit the decision was made that Natalie should go home.

When this happened she was home for one day before she went missing and was subsequently re-admitted to the short-stay residential unit where she remained for five months before being moved to a long-term residential care unit.

Sally and Jane were now extremely concerned about her future and wanted to be fully involved in planning meetings and reviews. To this end, although this meant having to take time off work, they attended several day-time meetings. It became increasingly difficult for them to have time off work, and they raised this with the social worker. They were told that meetings could only be held during office hours, which meant that thereafter only Sally could attend the meetings.

Over a period of time, Sally became increasingly confused about the plans being suggested for Natalie – the social worker seemed to want

Natalie to return home, whereas the officer-in-charge of the residential unit suggested she should remain in care. A meeting to resolve the issue was arranged, and Natalie requested that her mother attend. Sally was unable to take time off work and asked for the meeting to be rearranged, but it went ahead without Sally and Jane being present. They requested minutes of the meeting, but these never materialised.

While she was in the long-term unit, Natalie had overheard and challenged many derogatory comments made about lesbians and gay men. She told her key worker that her mother was lesbian and that the comments had upset her. In order to put a stop to their comments, Natalie asked if the staff could explain to the other young residents that there was nothing wrong with lesbians and gay men. The key worker advised her to keep quiet and not to tell anyone about her mother being a lesbian.

No formal agreement had been made about contact arrangements for Natalie and her family. At the last review 18 months ago, Sally and Jane were not invited to attend. However, Natalie frequently visited home to see her mother and Jane; and gradually the situation improved, and they all seemed to get on well together.

Natalie, now almost 16 years of age, is still in care.

Trainers' notes

In using this case study, it is important to recognise that some of the comments from participants may refer solely to the examples of bad practice. This argument could be expanded on in the following ways:

1   If this had been the usual practice of the social worker in regard to heterosexual families, would complaints not have been forwarded to the department?
2   Discuss the assumptions made about the family which involved only the biological mother.
3   Were those involved in working with Natalie, relying on a heterosexist definition of the family?
4   Consider the deliberate exclusion of Sally and Jane from reviews/planning meetings.
5   Why the change in plans for Natalie?
6   The Children Act 1989 stresses the importance of working in partnership with parents and other significant adults: e.g. if in the case of Sally and Jane, the mother had been cohabiting with a Schedule 1 offender, would he have been excluded from the

proceedings? In that heterosexual scenario he would more than likely have been invited to attend and allowed supervised access to Natalie. What does this say about assumptions made about lesbian mothers?

7   Did the non-validation of the lesbian relationship as an acceptable/alternative way of life, lead to assumptions being made about their child rearing ability and reinforce the blame/guilt that Sally already felt?

8   Natalie was left with unspoken negative messages about her family. Therefore she is 'abnormal'; mother is 'abnormal'.

9   Consider the lack of acknowledgement of Sally's feelings as a lesbian mother and her concern about her other children being 'taken away'.

10   Reinforcement by the residential worker that homosexuality is wrong and his/her unwillingness to challenge comments that were made by other residents in the unit.

11   What interest did the officer-in-charge have in this case? Whose needs were being met? Why did the officer-in-charge feel that care was the best place for Natalie? Is the officer-in-charge homophobic?

12   Why were there no review meetings held to discuss Natalie for over 18 months?

13   What policies should the residential unit have in relation to oppressive/discriminatory language?

Exercise   Lesbian mothers

Aim/purpose

- To think about the issues concerning gay or lesbian parents and how these might be addressed within a framework of anti-oppressive practice in social work.

Time

45 minutes.

Resources

- Copies of relevant newspaper cuttings as handouts.
- Flip chart, paper and pens.

Task

- Ask participants to read the material (10 minutes).
- Divide up into small groups of three to four people in order to consider the relevant issues.
- List some of the difficulties which may be encountered by lesbian/gay parents in general.
- Share ideas about anti-oppressive practice at an organisational, team and individual level.
- Record comments/information on flip chart (30 minutes).

Notes

- Depending on your knowledge of the group, consider how best to involve lesbian/gay participants who, in some situations, may wish to form a small group together.
- This material could also be adapted for use in teaching aimed at looking at the family, parenting, etc. – allowing participants to consider key elements of these concepts.

Exercise   'Coming out'

Aim/purpose

- To consider issues related to a worker's decision to come out.

Time

60 minutes.

Resources

- Copies of the case study of Sue on pages 101–2.
- Copies of 'Questions for discussion' on page 102.
- 'Trainers' notes' on pages 102–4.

Task

- Participants divide into groups of four to six people. Each person is given a copy of the case study and the questions for discussion.
- Participants read the case study, begin to discuss each question and provide answers.

- Each group selects one question that the group disagreed about.
- Participants re-form into large group.
- Each small group to present one aspect of this case that they found most difficult to address and/or agree on.

General issues

- Encourage constructive feedback.
- Trainer to be sensitive to individuals in the group who may have personal experience of legal discrimination.

Case study of Sue

Sue works in a community centre and is responsible for the parent and toddler group, which meets several mornings every week. She has worked there for the past year, enjoys her work and is very popular with the children and gets on well with their carers. Sue has a three-year-old son who occasionally attends the centre.

For the past four years Sue has been in a lesbian relationship and is very open about this outside of work. However, she has not disclosed her lesbianism to any of her colleagues at work. Sometimes they tell lesbian and gay jokes or refer to people as 'poofs' or 'queers'. At these times, Sue either stays silent or leaves the room.

Sue has decided that she wants to talk openly at work about her partner and thinks that a good starting point in her 'coming out' would be to display a range of photographs of her own family above her desk, as well as pictures of other diverse family groups.

Nothing is said until the next time her son attends the centre. Standing with another child, he points to a photograph of Sue and her partner and says, 'look, this is my mummy and my other mummy'.

Gradually over the following week fewer women attend the group. One day, one of the carers, called Pat, approaches Sue and says that the other mothers have stayed away because they have heard from their children that Sue is a lesbian and is living with another woman. Because of this they don't want her near their children. Pat says she personally does not believe that Sue is a lesbian because she has seen pictures of lesbians in the paper and Sue does not look like them. Sue responds by saying that she is.

That evening Sean, her manager, rings Sue at home because he has just had a phone call from the chairperson of the management committee who explains about Sue being a lesbian and that it is not appropriate for her to continue working with the toddler group. The chairperson also demanded that Sean 'do something about it' immediately.

Sean tells Sue that what she does with her life is not a problem for him personally; however, he has to think of the committee's views and the feelings of those who use the centre. He then explains that in view of Sue's good work record, he has been able to persuade the management committee to let her transfer to another centre where she will be working with a residents group – this is on the condition that Sue keeps her private life to herself.

Questions for discussion

1   Why has Sue not come out at the centre before now?
2   Why might she want to come out at work?
3   Why does Sue want to raise the children's awareness about lesbian relationships?
4   List any messages about homosexuality Sue might have received and internalised as a child.
5   In what sense is Sue's lesbianism irrelevant to her work?
6   In what way is Sue's lesbianism relevant to her work?
7   How might Sue have felt about some carers choosing not to attend the parent and toddler group?
8   Should Sue accept Sean's offer of a job in another centre? If you think she should accept the offer, on what grounds? If you think she should refuse his offer, what are your reasons?
9   Is Sean being supportive of Sue or not. In what ways?
10 What support will Sue need to say in her job?
11 Are there any other issues or comments you might want to make that arise from this case study?

Trainers' notes

1   Why has Sue not come out at the centre before now?

  ● Internalised oppression.
  ● Homophobia within the organisation.
  ● Homophobic response to lesbian mothers.

2   Why might she want to come out at work?

  ● To build more open and honest relationships.

- To end the need to lead a double life.
- To challenge homophobia.

3　Why does Sue want to raise the children's awareness about lesbian relationships?

- To promote an understanding of relationships and difference.
- Desire for her own child to feel positive.

4　List any messages about homosexuality Sue might have received and internalised as a child.

- Sick.
- Immoral/sinful.
- Unnatural.
- Men haters.
- Butch.

5　In what sense is Sue's lesbianism irrelevant to her work?

- Irrelevent to the quality of her practice.
- Personal lifestyle irrelevant.

6　In what way is Sue's lesbianism relevant to her work?

- Relevant in terms of anti-oppressive practice.
- Providing a positive role model.
- Possible presence of other lesbians.

7　How might Sue have felt about some carers choosing not to attend the parent and toddler group?

- A mixture of emotions; hurt, oppressed, relieved, threatened.

8　Should Sue accept Sean's offer of a job in another centre?

- Not on the conditions outlined, although Sue needs to have control over the decisions that affect her life.

8a   If you think she should accept the offer, on what grounds?

- Can work openly as a lesbian and is supported.

8b   If you think she should refuse his offer, what are your reasons?

- He is being discriminatory and oppressive in suggesting that she should leave.

9   Is Sean being supportive of Sue or not. In what ways?

- Over all, no. Sean is avoiding the issues and therefore feeding homophobia.

10   What support will Sue need to stay in her job?

- Clear statement made to service users and staff about anti-heterosexist practice and policies.
- Staff training.
- Support from other lesbians, e.g. consultant.

11   Are there any other issues or comments you might want to make that arise from this case study?

- Consider the physical environment of the centre and the availability of relevant posters, books, etc.
- The need for clearly worked out policies in work places.

References

Aggleton, P. et al. (1990), *AIDS: Working with Young People*, A training pack, Avert.

Ahmed, B. (1990), *Black Perspectives in Social Work*, Birmingham: Venture Press.

Brechin, A., Walmsley, J. and Gunn, M. (1989), *Sex and the Mentally Handicapped: A Lawyer's View in Making Connections*, London: Hodder & Stoughton.

Bremner, J. and Hillin, A. (1993), *Sexuality, Young People and Care*, London: CCETSW.

Campbell, B. (1988), *Unofficial Secrets*, London: Virago.

Caplan, P. (1987), *The Cultural Construction of Sexuality*, London: Routledge.

Central Council for Education and Training in Social Work (1993), *Positive Steps: Developing and Delivering Services to Black People Affected by HIV and AIDS*, London: CCETSW.

Central Council for Education and Training in Social Work (1995a), *Assuring Quality in the Diploma in Social Work – 1: Rules and Requirements for the DipSW*, Paper 30 (revised), London: CCETSW.

Central Council for Education and Training in Social Work (1995b), *Practice Teaching Awards* (Draft 3), Text for Paper 26.4, London: CCETSW.

Cosis Brown, H. (1992), 'Lesbians, the State and Social Work Practice' in Langan, M. and Day, L. (eds), *Women, Oppression and Social Work*, London: Routledge.

Davis, P. (1992), 'The Role of Disclosure in Coming Out Among Gay Men' in Plummer, K. (ed.), *Modern Homosexualities*, London: Routledge.

De Crescenzo, T. and McGill, C. (1978), 'Homophobia: A Study of the Attitudes of Mental Health Professionals Toward Homosexuality', unpublished thesis cited in Dulaney and Kelly (1982).

Department of Health (1990), Consultation Paper No. 16: *Foster Placement (Guidance and Regulations)*, London: HMSO.

Department of Health (1991), *The Children Act 1989 – Guidance and Regulations, Vol. 3, Family Placements*, London: HMSO.

Department of Health (1993), *Adoption: The Future*, London: HMSO.

Dominelli, L. (1988), *Anti-racist Social Work: A Challenge for White Practitioners and Educators*, London: Macmillan.

Dominelli, L. and McCleod, E. (1989), *Feminist Social Work*, London: Macmillan.

Dulaney, D. and Kelly, J. (1982), 'Improving Services to Gay and Lesbian Clients', *Social Work*, Vol. 27, No. 2, March.

Ely, P. and Denney, D. (1987), *Social Work in a Multi-racial Society*, Aldershot: Gower.

Evans, D. (1989/90), 'Section 28: Law, Myth and Paradox', *Critical Social Policy*, Vol. 9, No. 27.

Fierstein, H. (1989), *Torch Song Trilogy* (video).

Finklehor, D. and associates (eds) (1986), *A Sourcebook on Child Sexual Abuse*, London: Sage.

Garber, L. (ed.) (1994), *Tilting the Tower*, London: Routledge.

Gilchrist, J. and Trotter, J. (1996), 'Measuring Outcomes in Practice Learning and Assessment of Lesbian and Gay Issues in Social Work Training', *Social Work Education*, Vol. 15, No. 1.

Gittens, D. (1993), *The Family in Question* (2nd edn), London: Macmillan.

Gonczi, J., Hager, P. and Athanasou, J. (1993), *The Development of Competency-based Assessment Strategies for Professions*, National Office of Overseas Skills Recognition, Research Paper No. 8, DEET, Canberra: Australian Government Publishing Service.

Gooding, C. (1992), *Trouble with the Law: A Legal Handbook for Lesbians and Gay Men*, London: GMP Publishers.

Gramich, J. (1988), 'Homophobia: A New Challenge!', *Social Work*, Vol. 28, March/April.

Hager, P., Gonczi, A. and Athanasou, J. (1994), 'General Issues about Assessment of Competence in Assessment and Evaluation', *Higher Education*, Vol. 19, No. 1.

Hanmer, J. and Statham, D. (1988), *Women and Social Work: Towards a Women-Centred Practice*, London: Macmillan.

Hawkins, P. and Shohet, R. (1989), *Supervision in the Helping Professions: An Individual and Organisational Approach*, Oxford: Oxford University Press.

Hicks, S. (1993), 'Adoption: The Experiences of Lesbians and Gay Men in Fostering and Adoption: A study of the impact of the process of assessment upon prospective carers', unpublished MA thesis, University of Manchester.

Hillin, A. (1985), 'When You Stop Hiding Your Sexuality!', *Social Work Today*, 4 November.

Honey, A. and Mumford, P. (1986), *The Manual of Learning Styles* (2nd edn), Maidenhead: Peter Honey Publishers.

Jordan, B. (1991), 'Competencies and Values', *Social Work Education*, Vol. 10, No. 1.

Jordan, B., Kazi, M., Karban, K., Masson, H. and O'Byrne, P. (1993), 'Teaching Values: An Experience of the Diploma in Social Work', *Social Work Education*, Vol. 12, No. 1.

Keating, A.L. (1994), 'Teaching the Sexual Others', in Garber, L. (ed.), *Tilting the Tower*, London: Sage.

Kitzinger, C. (1987), *The Social Construction of Lesbianism*, Englewood Cliffs, NJ: Prentice Hall International.

Kolb, A., Rubin, I.M. and McIntyre, J.M. (1974), *Emotional Psychology: An Experimental Approach*, Englewood Cliffs, NJ: Prentice Hall International.

Logan, J. and Kershaw, S. (1994), 'Heterosexism and Social Work Education: The Invisible Challenge', *Social Work Education*, Vol. 13, No. 2.

Lorde, A. (1984), *Sister Outsider*, New York: Crossing Press.

McMillan, S. (1989), 'Lesbians and Gay Men Need Services Too', *Social Work Today*, 4 July.

Mills, S. (1995), 'Creating a Safe Environment in Residential Care', in Stone, K. and Vallender, I. (eds), *Spinning Plates: Practice Teaching and Learning for Residential Child Care Initiative*, London: CCETSW.

National Association of Local Government Officers (1992), *Lesbian and Gay Organising Handbook*, London: NALGO.

National Association of Probation Officers (1989), *Working with Lesbians and Gay Men as Clients of the Service: Good Practice Guidelines*, London: NAPO.

National Institute of Social Work (1995), *Working in the Social Services*, London: NISW.

Nottingham Council for Voluntary Services (1989), Extract from equal opportunities document cited in Ward, D. & Mullender, A. (1991).

Phillipson, J. (1992), *Practising Equality: Men, Women and Social Work*, London: CCETSW.

Richards, M. (1988), 'Developing the Context of Practice Teaching (Part 1)', in Phillipson, J., Richards, M. and Sawdon, D., *Towards a Practice Led Curriculum*, London: NISW.

Robinson, V. (1993), 'Heterosexuality: Beginnings and Connections', in Wilkinson, S. and Kitzinger, C. (eds), *Heterosexuality: A Feminism and Psychology Reader*, London: Sage.

Schoenberg, R. and Goldberg, R.S. (1984), *Homosexuality and Social Work*, New York: Haworth Press.

Skeates, J. and Jabri, D. (eds) (1988), *Fostering and Adoption by Lesbians and Gay Men*, London: Strategic Policy Unit.

Tasker, F. and Golombok, S. (1991), 'Children Raised by Lesbian Mothers: The Empirical Evidence', *Family Law*, 21 May.

Tatchell, P. (1992), 'Equal Rights for All', in Plummer, K. (ed.), *Modern Homosexualities*, London: Routledge.

Thompson, N. (1993), *Anti-Discriminatory Practice*, London: Macmillan.

Trenchard, L. and Warren, H. (1984), *Something To Tell You*, London Gay Teenage Group, London: Trojan Press.

Trotter, J. and Gilchrist, J. (1995), 'Assessing DipSW Students: Anti-discriminatory Practice in Relation to Lesbian and Gay Issues', unpublished.

Ward, D.A. and Mullender, A. (1991), 'Empowerment and Oppression: An Indissoluble Pairing for Contemporary Social Work', *Critical Social Policy*, No. 2.

Webb, R. and Tossell, D. (1991), *Social Issues for Carers*, London: Edward Arnold.

Weeks, J. (1989), *Sex, Politics and Society: The Regulation of Sexuality since 1800*, Harlow: Longman.

Weeks, J. (1991), *Against Nature: Essays on History, Sexuality and Identity*, London: Rivers Oram Press.

Wilkinson, S. and Kitzinger, C. (1993), *Heterosexuality: A Feminism and Psychology Reader*, London: Sage.

Winterson, J. (1987), *Oranges Are Not the Only Fruit*, London: Pandora Press.

Wisniewski, J. and Toomey, B. (1987), 'Are Social Workers Homophobic?', *Social Work*, Vol. 32, No. 5, September/October.

Index

CONFRONTING PREJUDICE

Southampton
SOLENT
University

MOUNTBATTEN LIBRARY
Tel: 023 8031 9249

Please return this book no later than the date stamped.
Loans may usually be renewed - in person, by phone,
or via the web OPAC. Failure to renew or return on time
may result in an accumulation of penalty points.

− 6 DEC 2007		